NOTES

including
- *Life of the Author*
- *The Transcendentalist Movement*
- *Introduction to* Walden
- *Summaries and Commentaries*
- *Extra-Literary Recognition of Thoreau*
- *Essay Questions and Theme Topics*
- *Selected Bibliography*

by
Joseph R. McElrath, Jr., Ph.D.
Department of English
State University of New York at Brockport

INCORPORATED
LINCOLN, NEBRASKA 68501

Editor

Gary Carey, M.A.
University of Colorado

Consulting Editor

James L. Roberts, Ph.D.
Department of English
University of Nebraska

Cliffs Notes, Inc.   Lincoln, Nebraska

CONTENTS

Walden Notes

LIFE OF THE AUTHOR

Henry David Thoreau was born on July 12, 1817, of rather ordinary parents in Concord, outside of Boston, Massachusetts. His childhood and adolescence, from what little is known about these periods of his life, appear to have been typical for the time. Thoreau attended the Concord Academy as an undistinguished student, and when he was sixteen, his father, a pencil manufacturer, had saved enough money to send him to Harvard. There he read a great deal and thus philosophically and literarily prepared himself to become a spokesman for the transcendentalist movement; again, however, his career as a student was unspectacular.

When Thoreau graduated from Harvard in 1837, he had been educated for four possible professions: law, the clergy, business, or teaching. He was really interested in none of these professions for which he had been prepared, but he tried teaching for a short while. He was given a position in Concord, but soon resigned when he discovered that he was expected to teach by conscientiously beating the ABC's into his students with a rod. He decided that he would rather make pencils with his father and do some occasional surveying. (The latter activity would later come to be one of the main bread-and-butter occupations of his life.) Needless to say, the townspeople were surprised that a Harvard man should turn out so disappointingly. This was to be the first of many ways in which Thoreau would rebel against society's expectations for him.

Yet, while the townspeople were looking upon him as a loafer, Thoreau was then, in the late 1830s and early 1840s, mapping out his strategy to become as famous and influential a transcendentalist writer and lecturer as Emerson. He tried teaching again in 1838 with his brother John, and they conducted what today would still be considered a progressive school. But this was only a tangential interest for him; he had already decided what his primary vocation would be. In 1837, he had begun his journal, the workbook to which he would practically devote his life and in which he would perfect his art. Until his death in 1862, Thoreau religiously worked day in and day out at this occupation that the scoffing townspeople were ignorant of. To realize the intense seriousness with which he pursued it, one can profitably read through his journal of 1838. There one finds the anxiety of the struggling, would-be master craftsman whose work does not yet meet his own standards of excellence:

> But what does all this scribbling amount to? What is now scribbled in the heat of the moment one can contemplate with somewhat of satisfaction, but alas! tomorrow — aye, tonight — it is stale, flat and unprofitable — in fine, is not; only its shell remains like some red parboiled lobster shell which, kicked aside ever so often, still stares at you in the path.

In short, Thoreau was deadly serious when he took up his pen — so serious that, as was usual with Thoreau, he probably revised and polished the above complaint several times before he entered it in his journal.

During the time that Thoreau and his brother were conducting their academy, they went on a boat trip (1839) that was to provide the raw material which Thoreau would work into his first book, *A Week on the Concord and Merrimack Rivers* (1849). It was ten years between the actual river voyage and when his highly idealistic celebration of it was published. During that time, Thoreau read, wrote, and worked at whatever jobs he could find. He surveyed, made pencils with his father, and did odd jobs when he needed the money — thus leaving him plenty of time for his journal. In 1841, Thoreau moved into the Emerson household as the family's handyman. He made much use of Emerson's library, and a warm relationship grew between them as they daily conversed and as Thoreau began to submit poems and essays to the *Dial*, the transcendentalist journal that Emerson edited. (Most of these poems and essays were later

included in *A Week on the Concord and Merrimack Rivers.*)
Emerson came to admire Thoreau so much that he allowed him
to edit the entire April, 1843, issue.

Emerson had high ambitions for his young friend and, in
1843, he arranged for Thoreau to stay with his brother, William
Emerson, on Staten Island so that he might make contacts with
New York publishers. Unfortunately, this attempt to find publication was a failure, and Thoreau soon returned to Concord and
resumed work on his journal. Then in March, 1845, he initiated
what was to be the most significant event of his life: he borrowed
an ax and began to construct a cabin on Emerson's land by the
north shore of Walden Pond.

He moved into his cabin on July 4, 1845, and, as *Walden*
indicates, he attempted to reduce his needs to the barest essentials of life and to establish an intimate, spiritual relationship
with nature.

For Thoreau, living at Walden Pond was a noble experiment
in three ways. First, Thoreau was intent upon resisting the
debilitating effects of the industrial revolution (division of
labor, the mind-dulling repetition of factory work, and a material-
ist vision of life). The Walden experiment allowed him to "turn
back the clock" to the simpler, agrarian way of life that was
quickly disappearing in New England. Second, by reducing his
expenditures, he reduced the time necessary to support himself,
and thus he could devote more time to the perfection of his art.
While at the pond, he was able to write most of *A Week on the
Concord and Merrimack Rivers.* And third, he and Emerson had
asserted that one can most easily experience the Ideal, or the
Divine, through nature; at Walden Pond, Thoreau was able to
test continually the validity of this theory by living closely, day-
to-day, with nature.

Thoreau left the pond in 1847, and when Emerson went to
England in the fall of that year, Thoreau once again joined the
household to look after the family's needs. Upon Emerson's
return in 1848, Thoreau moved back to his parents' home where
he remained until his death.

Between 1847 and 1854, Thoreau spent his time walking through the countryside, making pencils, surveying, and devoting himself to a new passion: the composition of *Walden*. The work went through many painstaking revisions during those seven years; yet when it appeared, the product of those years of labor was not well received. While it was not so great a failure as *A Week on the Concord and Merrimack Rivers* (275 sold; 75 given away), and while it did receive some good reviews, it hardly fulfilled Thoreau's dream of becoming a major spokesman for the transcendentalist movement. He did not complain about the poor reception given to *Walden,* but it must have been a major psychological setback. Viewed today, its publication marked the high point of his career, and his contemporaries virtually ignored it.

Thoreau's later years were characterized by an increased interest in the cause of abolition and the scientific study of nature. In 1844, he wrote an essay entitled "Herald of Freedom," which praised abolitionist Wendell Phillips, and in 1849 he published "Civil Disobedience," which also dealt with the subject of slavery in America. In neither piece did Thoreau protest loudly, but in 1854, his indignation began to grow when he delivered a speech entitled "Slavery in Massachusetts." He became more involved with the abolitionist movement, and in 1859 delivered his fiery "Plea for Captain John Brown," wherein he praised the morality of Brown's violent resistance to slavery and sternly denounced the federal government for sanctioning the institution of slavery. This speech was soon followed by another entitled "The Last Days of John Brown." In 1844, Thoreau had advocated non-violent, passive resistance to slavery, but as it became more and more a central concern of his life, he gradually came to advocate armed revolt, even civil war, as a valid means of destroying an immoral system.

In his abolitionist speeches and essays, Thoreau revealed a turbulent sense of outrage. That was one side of his personality. The other side, as seen when he was in the presence of nature, also remained strong during his later years. And as he grew weaker after his bouts with tuberculosis in 1851 and 1855, he turned to nature in order to regain his health—but not with the transcendentalist fervor that characterized his youth. During this period of decline, his journal reveals a growing interest in natural history accompanied by a more "scientific," less transcendental, approach to nature. Although the latter part of his journal does contain many imaginative descriptions of nature similar to those found in *Walden,* there is an increasing number of entries like the following of 1860:

> It rained hard on the twentieth and part of the following night—two and one eighth inches of rain in all, there being no drought—raising the river from some two or three inches above summer level to seven and a half inches above the summer level at 7 A.M. of the twenty-first.

Such entries have led some scholars to think that Thoreau gradually "decayed" as a transcendentalist during the late 1850s and early 1860s.

On May 6, 1862, Thoreau died in his parents' home in Concord. A man of admirable spirit, he passed out of the world with typical Thoreauvian humor: when a friend asked him if he had made amends with God, Thoreau quipped, "I did not know that we had ever quarreled."

When Thoreau died, scarcely anyone in America noticed, and the few that did mourn his passing would have been surprised to learn that, a century later, he would be unanimously acknowledged as one of America's greatest literary artists. George W. Curtis did not understate the matter when he wrote in Thoreau's obituary that "the name of Henry Thoreau is known to very few persons beyond those who personally knew him." Thoreau had fervently devoted himself to the pursuit of a literary career in the late 1830s, but after thirty years of intense effort in his art, he died a failure by contemporary standards of success. In his eulogy at Thoreau's funeral, Emerson declared that "the country knows not yet, or in the least part, how great a son it has lost," and it was not until the twentieth century was well under way that Thoreau came to be recognized as the genius that he was.

What little recognition Thoreau did receive during the latter half of the nineteenth century was strongly colored by some unfortunate remarks made by Emerson and James Russell Lowell, two very influential men in matters of literary taste. Both men published essays on Thoreau shortly after his death and virtually determined for quite some time what the public's attitude toward Thoreau would be. While supposedly eulogizing Thoreau, Emerson managed to emphasize every negative trait that he had found (or imagined) in Thoreau's personality. One sees in his portrait of Thoreau an almost inhuman ascetic and stoic ("He had no temptations to fight against—no appetites, no passions, no taste for elegant trifles") and a somewhat cranky, anti-social hermit ("Few lives contained so many renunciations. . . . It cost him nothing to say No; indeed, he found it much easier than to say Yes"). In this eulogy, Emerson also strongly emphasized Thoreau's abilities as a naturalist, and thus established the image of Thoreau-the-nature-lover (in the worst sense of the term) that was to obscure his primary significance as an artist for quite some time. Three years later, in 1865, James Russell Lowell published his essay on Thoreau, and reinforced Emerson's caricature of Thoreau as a cold, brittle, anti-social recluse. He wrote that Thoreau "seems to me to have been a man with so high a conceit of himself that he accepted without questioning, and insisted on accepting, his defects and weaknesses of character as virtues and powers peculiar to himself. . . . His mind strikes us as cold and wintry." This was a damning indictment, but even more detrimental to Thoreau's reputation was Lowell's assertion that Thoreau was merely a minor Emerson, an imitator of his mentor. In *A Fable for Critics*, Lowell depicted a Thoreau who trod "in Emerson's tracks with legs painfully short." In addition, he opened the essay on Thoreau with a similar gibe:

> Among the pistillate plants kindled to fruitage by the Emersonian pollen, Thoreau is thus far the most remarkable; and it is something eminently fitting that his posthumous works should be offered us by Emerson, for they are strawberries from his own garden.

To realize the influence that Lowell's opinion carried in literary circles, one should note that as late as 1916 Mark Van Doren reiterated a similar misconception in his *Henry David Thoreau.* Van Doren wrote that "Thoreau is a specific Emerson" and that, philosophically, Thoreau's position was "almost identical with Emerson's."

To those familiar with Emerson's and Thoreau's writings, such a view of an "Emersonian Thoreau" is a gross misconception. Philosophically and aesthetically, they were often at odds, and one need only read Emerson's *Nature* and Thoreau's *Walden* to note the differences in personality and, most important, the differences in their art. Yet, the "Emersonian" tag hindered the recognition of Thoreau's unique greatness for over half a century, as did the popular conceptions of the effete "nature lover" and the cranky hermit. One finds, for example, Oliver Wendell Holmes treating Thoreau as a joke: "Thoreau, the nullifier of civilization . . . insisted on nibbling his asparagus at the wrong end." And Robert Louis Stevenson echoed Lowell by terming Thoreau "dry, priggish, and selfish," adding that "it was not inappropriate, surely, that he had much close relations with the fish."

The ill-founded jokes began to come to an end during the 1890s when serious scholars began to take a closer look at the basis of Thoreau's small reputation. The portraits of Thoreau by Emerson and Lowell were re-examined and most critics came to the conclusion that, as Charles C. Abbot wrote in 1895, "neither Emerson nor Lowell was fitted to the task they undertook." Emerson's journals revealed a basic misunderstanding of Thoreau's aims and accomplishments; Lowell, the "in-door, kid-glove critic," was obviously out of touch with the thorny world that Thoreau inhabited. Between the 1890s and the mid-twentieth century, the old misconceptions about Thoreau withered away, and as critics began examining Thoreau on his own ground—that is, his writings—his reputation grew rapidly. Today, his reputation as an artist is greater than Emerson's and, ironically, virtually no one except specialists in American literature reads either Lowell's poetry or his literary criticism. As Wendell Glick has noted: "One of the most conspicuous nails in the coffin of Lowell's reputation is his maligning of Thoreau's genius." By the unanimous consent of literary critics, "genius" is the only word to describe the once unappreciated artist of a small town in Massachusetts.

THE TRANSCENDENTALIST MOVEMENT

Henry Thoreau once declared that he "was born in the nick of time." This statement may puzzle or startle the reader when he first encounters it, but it should be noted as one of the most significant sentences Thoreau ever wrote. To a great degree, the character of Thoreau's life and the very production of *Walden* were results of his birth date. In 1817, the transcendentalist movement, for which Thoreau was destined to be one of the major spokesmen, was born. It would become, by the late 1830s, the intellectual force that charged Thoreau's imagination and channeled his energies into a vocation of writing and lecturing about the possibilities of an ideal existence for man. While Thoreau was not very interested in the immediate concerns that initiated the transcendentalist movement, men like Orestes Brownson, Bronson Alcott, and Emerson, who had been in the movement since the 1820s, strongly attracted the young Harvard graduate of 1837 and virtually forged the shape of his mature life.

One would not know it from Thoreau's writings, but the transcendentalist movement was the result of a heated religious controversy within the Unitarian church. It began in the 1820s with a revolt of the younger clergymen in and around Boston. They were protesting what Emerson termed "the corpse-cold Unitarianism of Harvard College and Brattle Street." They saw in Unitarianism a form of religion that had lost the ability to fulfill the spiritual and emotional needs of worshippers because of its hyper-rational approach to Christianity. To these young clergymen, Unitarianism had removed the essentials of genuine religious experience—intuition, feeling, and mystery—and had replaced them with a rationalistic, common-sense, "rule-book" approach to the religious life. The Calvinists, with their rigorous beliefs, had charged that it was not a religion at all, but merely a

Sunday morning social gathering for businessmen who did not wish to be troubled about the ethics of their everyday dealings. And although the optimistically-inclined transcendentalists had little in common with the Calvinists, they agreed with this assessment of Unitarian complacency in spiritual matters. In one sense, the transcendentalists were like the Calvinists: they lamented the loss of the deeply felt experience of God and the rigorous morality that had characterized faith in New England before the rise of Unitarianism. Orestes Brownson spoke for quite a few young clergymen when he termed Unitarianism "the jumping-off place from the church to absolute infidelity."

The root of the problem was the eighteenth-century philosophical view of man that had molded the character of the Unitarian church. It was the "common sense," or "sensational," philosophy popularized by John Locke. One of its major tenets was that the mind at birth is like a blank tablet and that all knowledge results from filling this tablet with ideas and impressions *as they are received through the five senses.* Hence, to change the metaphor, the mind was seen as a sort of mechanical organizer limited to the function of receiving information through sensory channels and classifying it into proper categories. (For those to whom this concept is new, it might help to visualize the Lockean mind in two other ways: as a sort of file cabinet in which ideas are placed and stored for future use; or, as a camera within which impressions from the external world are received and preserved.) With such an image of man's mind as a passive receptor of impressions and limited to what knowledge comes through sensory experience, the Unitarian church formulated a common-sense religion whereby being religious was simply a matter of learning (receiving) God's laws through reading the scriptures (sensory experience), listening to the sermons (sensory experience), and seeing God's handiwork in nature (sensory experience). It was thought that since man's knowledge is limited by his senses, he can never directly experience or know the *super*sensory (the supernatural) God; as a result, man's only possible religious activity is to learn and believe what his senses reveal to him about God, and his only duty is to conform to what scripture and the church teach as God's will.

Hence, one can see the dry, rule-book nature of Unitarianism: God was "out there," removed from the sensory experience of man; the miraculous aspect of Christianity was played down since miracles cannot be verified by common sense; and the emphasis on man being a rational creature precluded concern for the irrational nature of an emotional or intuitional experience of God. To the transcendentalists, the vitals had been removed from Christianity, and they revolted.

To know God at second hand, through the church and scripture, was not enough; and Emerson, who eventually left the ministry, made this clear when he addressed the Harvard graduating class of 1838. He declared to an audience made up of many clergymen and students for the Unitarian ministry that they should not let any institutional church, dogma, creed, or even Christ himself, stand in the way of their *direct* communication with God. This was a radical declaration, but a logical one for Emerson who had in the previous years formulated a belief in man's ability to attain supersensory knowledge and to experience the supernatural.

For the student of Thoreau's *Walden*, the key point behind Emerson's "Divinity School Address" is a view of man that denies the Lockean image of the mind. Emerson and the other transcendentalists asserted that man is not limited to simply learning *about* God; rather than being only a *receiver* of sense impressions, man's mind is also a faculty that can *create*, independent of the senses, a consciousness of God. Contrary to Locke's "blank tablet," the mind is a potentially powerful instrument capable of imagination and intuition, and capable of establishing personal communion with the divine.

In the late eighteenth and early nineteenth centuries, German transcendentalist philosophers such as Kant, Fichte, and Schelling had originally proposed this view of the "creative intellect." And the English romantic poet Coleridge had popularized it in his country before Emerson and his fellow transcendentalists made it the core idea of their intellectual revolution in New England. It had arrived in America "in the nick of time,"

when an intellectually and spiritually hungry Thoreau graduated from Harvard in 1837 looking for a way of life, a cause, a
philosophy, anything worth devoting his life to. There, waiting
for him, were the New England transcendentalists with their
vitally new and exciting vision of man's capabilities. Since this
vision is the core of *Walden,* a further word should be said about
these extraordinary capabilities that Emerson claimed for man.

Years before the "Divinity School Address" of 1838, Emerson had decided that man creates a consciousness of God —
"God" being the spiritual force that he also termed the "over-
soul" or the "ideal." If, Emerson reasoned, man creates consciousness of the divine, then, in effect, he creates the divine. If
he intellectually creates the divine, then he possesses a divine
power and must thus be divine himself. Accordingly, in *Nature*
(1836), Emerson described the individual who does not realize
this god-like power of consciousness within himself as "a god in
ruins." (Thoreau used a phrase very similar to Emerson's in the
"Winter Animals" chapter of *Walden;* there, the men who are
unconscious of the divinity in them are termed "defaced and
leaning monuments" of God.) He believed that each man,
through the potential power of his intellect, has the ability to
become god-like, to realize an ideal mode of existence, to raise
himself above (that is, transcend) his presently imperfect, unsatisfactory situation in life. In short, Emerson proposed to his
readers the possibility of total, ecstatic self-fulfillment; this was
what fired Thoreau's imagination. Years later it was what he
offered to his readers in *Walden:* "I do not mean to prescribe
rules to strong and valiant natures . . . but mainly to the mass of
men who are discontented, and idly complain of the hardness of
their lot or of the times, when they might improve them." With
the same optimism and faith in man's capabilities that Emerson
had, Thoreau told his audience, "I know of no more encouraging
fact than the unquestionable ability of man to elevate his life by
a conscious endeavor."

In *Walden,* Thoreau offers an example of one possible approach to realizing one's divinity, to fulfilling one's potential for
ideal existence in the real world. Like Emerson, he advises his

readers to exercise their minds and create an idea of themselves as they might ideally be, and then find the means of making that idea, or dream, come true. Thoreau made this explicit when, in the chapter "Economy," he wrote:

> When one man has reduced a fact of the imagination [the idea of one's ideal self as created by the mind] to be a fact of his understanding [a fact of everyday, concrete reality], I foresee that all men will at length establish their lives on that basis.

In the "Conclusion" chapter of *Walden*, Thoreau again makes this point and reassures his readers that, based upon his experience at Walden Pond, he believes that an ideal mode of life is within everyone's grasp:

> I learned this, at least, by my experiment; that if one advances confidently in the direction of his dreams, and endeavors to live the life which he has imagined, he will meet with a success unexpected in common hours. He will put some things behind, will pass an invisible boundary; new, universal, and more liberal laws will begin to establish themselves around and within him; or the old laws will be expanded, and interpreted in his favor in a more liberal sense, and he will live with the license of a hgher order of beings. . . . If you have built castles in the air, your work need not be lost; that is where they should be. Now put the foundations under them.

Walden proposes that men, to use a commonplace phrase, can and should "make the best of two worlds"— the supernatural world of the spirit and the natural world of everyday existence. Writers of an earlier century might have used the expression, "bringing God into the marketplace," to approximate what Thoreau was suggesting. In the terminology of his own intellectual milieu, Thoreau advises his readers to recognize the Ideal, and then design their lives accordingly so that the Ideal becomes the Real, so "the best of two worlds" may become "one world," wherein spiritual existence is the same as everyday existence.

Walden is the artistic depiction of the quest to realize such a state of life. Unlike Emerson, who usually wrote in theory about an experience of the ideal, Thoreau provided his contemporaries — and us — with a concrete way to attain successfully such a quest for a higher mode of life. In *Walden*, we vividly see Thoreau erect the "foundations" under his "castles in the air"; we see him create a way of life that enables him to make his dream of self-fulfillment come true.

Thus, as he attempts to "awaken" the spirit of dull John Field in *Walden*, Thoreau offers to us, his readers, an example of how we might "wake up" and *transcend* our own unsatisfactory lives. Fittingly for a transcendentalist, Thoreau offers us in *Walden* nothing less than the possibility of realizing our own perfection, our own divinity.

INTRODUCTION TO *WALDEN*

In some editions of *Walden*, there is included an inscription page which precedes the first chapter. On this page the narrator of *Walden* declares:

I DO NOT PROPOSE TO WRITE AN ODE TO DEJECTION, BUT TO BRAG AS LUSTILY AS CHANTICLEER IN THE MORNING, STANDING ON HIS ROOST, IF ONLY TO WAKE MY NEIGHBORS UP.

The reader attempting to approach an understanding and appreciation of *Walden* should immediately note that here, in this inscription, the germ of the book may be found. The tone is one of great confidence and joy; the pages to follow will be the narrator's optimistic proclamation of the richness and fullness of his life at Walden Pond. He will brag lustily, with a full-throated voice, that he, like the rooster that greets the dawn, has successfully created a way of living that has enabled him to find a "new day" in his life. It is a new world and a new self that he has discovered through his thought and activity at his woodland retreat. He feels as though he has been reborn into a fresh and new, more satisfying life; he celebrates the feeling of having left behind his old self, the spiritually-asleep creature made lifeless by "the dead dry life of society," for the sake of a new and ecstatic spiritual life.

In light of what has been said about Thoreau's transcendentalism, one might rightly expect *Walden* to begin on just such a note of buoyancy and high-spiritedness. This is a fitting way to begin the artistic depiction of *how* one man moved away from the state of being a "god in ruins" and moved toward a god-like state of fulfillment. Thus commences one of the most sophisticated and artistic "brags" in the history of American literature. And before the student decides to term the book the work of a rabid egomaniac, a further word about the nature of this "brag" should be offered.

In "The American Scholar," Emerson described the three basic stages of a transcendentalist's life: first, he learns all that is of merit in the wisdom of the past; second, he establishes a harmonious relationship with nature through which he is able to discover ethical truths and communicate with the divine. With these two stages, the transcendentalist has developed his higher faculties; he has cultivated his life and "spiritualized" it. (We see the narrator of *Walden* go through these two stages in his progress toward spiritual rebirth.) After thus cultivating his own spirit, the transcendentalist does not selfishly remain content with himself. The third stage he must attempt, after self-renewal, is the renewal of society-at-large. After being nurtured by books and nature, he must attempt to share his spiritual gains with other men who have not yet achieved their perfect spiritual states.

Walden may be viewed as Thoreau's attempt at this third stage in the transcendental life. In it, we hear the "bragging" narrator reiterating the firm conviction that all men may achieve the exhilaration that he feels. He vividly shows us his life; he "brags" of his achievement; and he tries by his example to renew "the dead dry life of society." Thus, when the narrator "brags," it is not only for himself but for all humanity's *potential* for greatness. Like the other transcendentalists, Thoreau was a strong moralist, and one of the most distinctive characteristics of *Walden* is that the narrator consistently tries to alert his readers to their potential for spiritual growth. So, while the narrator may crow loudly, sometimes proudly strutting about, and may boast of his "clear flame" with a degree of pride approaching *hubris,* it should not be forgotten that his self-pride is to be shared by his readers. If the narrator sometimes seems smug and self-righteous, it must be recalled that he is crowing "to wake his neighbors up" to *their* own greatness, not just his own.

The narrator's celebration of life and his call for all men to recognize the potential magnificence of life form the core idea, or unifying theme, of *Walden.* This point cannot be stressed too strongly because, for over a century, many individuals — sometimes very intelligent ones — have tended to ignore this centrally significant fact and have chosen to view *Walden* in other ways. While one considers the different aspects of *Walden,* these aspects should not obscure the essential core of the book: the process by which the narrator moves toward spiritual fulfillment.

The way in which the reader can keep this core foremost in his mind is to approach *Walden* as what it primarily is: a carefully contrived, closely-knit work of art with a poetic structure designed to support and restate the core idea. This may easily be done if the reader predisposes himself to two facts. The first is that, before anything else, Thoreau was an artist — an artist above and beyond being a devotee of nature, a naturalist, an economist, an anarchist, an abolitionist, or a philosopher. Since the 1930s, this is the key fact about Thoreau that has been established by scholars, and it has been the key factor in Thoreau's rise to prominence in American letters. *Walden* is the product of a man possessed with the idea of creating a great book. The second fact is that *Walden* was Thoreau's most successful attempt at creating art, to the degree that *Walden* exhibits the qualities of a great poem. If one traces the process by which Thoreau transformed his first version of *Walden* into the final version (this may be done by consulting J. Lyndon Shanley's *The Making of Walden*), he can see the work being changed from a rough report on pond-side living to a highly compressed, complex, and symbolic work of art.

Of course, one can grasp the central theme of *Walden* without taking too much note of the poetic structure of the work. If one takes the attitude that one critic has — that *"Walden* is a collection of eighteen essays recounting Thoreau's experience at Walden Pond, near Concord, Massachusetts, from July 4, 1845, to September 6, 1847" — it would still be possible to come to the theme of *Walden.* But to view the work as merely a collection of essays is to miss the rich texture that Thoreau gave the work as a whole. The organic, poetic unity, and the rich symbolic structure which Thoreau created in *Walden* is what makes it a work far superior to his other works which present almost identical themes. And it is only by being aware of the symbolic structure that one can discover how the fiction of Thoreau's *Walden* is ultimately autobiographical. It is through the symbolism that one comes to see that *Walden* is Thoreau's artistic projection of his most deeply felt shortcomings and needs — psychological needs that are fulfilled in the fiction that Thoreau's narrator lives.

The term "fiction" is used here to describe the *narrator's* record of what happened to him at Walden Pond. Both the "I" voice of the narrator and the world he describes must be distinguished from the real Thoreau and the world that he inhabited while writing *Walden. Walden* is a fiction, an imaginative creation; it is not a strict "autobiography" in the sense that we usually assign to that word. The "I" voice we hear bragging "as lustily as chanticleer in the morning" is Thoreau's representation of himself in 1854, as he would like to be, as he hopes to be someday. Or, it is an older Thoreau's representation of the ecstasy that he felt when he was younger. In writing *Walden,* he is seeking to assert and perhaps recapture his former happiness.

It should never be forgotten that seven years separated the actual experience at Walden Pond and the publication of *Walden.* As many critics have contended, those seven years witnessed Thoreau's loss of the intense inspiration and the ecstasy in nature that characterized his youth. In 1854, Thoreau was looking backward to his years of spiritual fulfillment before his highly subjective idealism had begun to wane. And he is hopefully looking forward to regaining it.

In short, *Walden* is a kind of wish book. With the "I" voice of *Walden*, Thoreau fabricates an ideal alter-ego, a wish-fulfillment figure, a character who is able to say the things about himself that Thoreau would like to be able to claim. In his youth, Thoreau felt a terrific sense of inspiration and wholeness whenever he was in the presence of nature. He believed that he had empirically proven the tenet of Emersonian idealism that the divine may be experienced through the medium of nature. In fact, Thoreau was so excited, so exhilarated by his sensual and spiritual experience of nature that he seriously entertained the idea that nature is actually God. He went past Emerson, who declared that nature is the symbol of the spiritual, and proposed that it is more than a mere symbol. In *A Week on the Concord and Merrimack Rivers*, Thoreau's idealism surpassed Emerson's when he wrote:

> May we not *see* God? Are we to be put off and amused in this life, as it were with mere allegory? Is not Nature, rightly read, that of which she is commonly taken to be the symbol merely?

Statements such as this caused Reverend George Ripley to denounce Thoreau's "pantheism." Nature fulfilled him to such a degree that he had to celebrate it as divine; so great was the physical and spiritual harmony between him and nature that he felt he was experiencing divinity. And it was to this state that he wanted to return in 1854. Hence, at the climax of the narrator's quest for harmony with nature in the "Spring" chapter, we find the "I" voice experiencing nature's expression of the divine. The ecstasy that the "I" voice brags of in this chapter is the ecstasy that Thoreau longs for. The spiritual rebirth that the narrator achieves in *Walden* is the goal toward which Thoreau was attempting to design his life in 1854.

SUMMARIES AND COMMENTARIES

CHAPTER ONE

Economy - Rebian

Summary

Walden begins with the narrator informing his audience that this book was written in answer to questions posed about his two-year stay at Walden Pond. He hopes to explain the spiritually rich life he enjoyed and, at the same time, through presenting the example of his own life, teach his readers something about the shortcomings and possibilities of theirs. While living at the pond, he had the opportunity to view society from the outside and see that, in contrast to his happy situation, most men "lead lives of quiet desperation." While continually perfecting his life by living simply and close to nature, he could see other men wasting their lives by frantically scurrying here and there, foolishly chasing after wealth and social status which could never fulfill their deepest needs. He can only regretfully conclude that modern man, obsessed with material gain, has "not leisure for a true integrity . . . he has not time to be anything but a machine." The narrator is especially saddened that even farming, an activity which allows men to live close to the spiritually elevating influences of nature, has lost its noble character and has become simply another enervating and dehumanizing way to accumulate wealth and property.

The narrator's stay at Walden taught him that no one need resign himself to a dreary, drudging life; no man has to be "so occupied with the factitious cares and superfluously coarse labors of life that its finer fruits cannot be plucked." The narrator found that all men may confidently hope for a better life. They need take only the first step toward perfection: self-criticism. For all men, there is hope *if* they are willing to take a critical view of their lives, as the narrator has so acutely done, and then set about reforming themselves.

The narrator believes that once a man critically reviews his life he will immediately discover a major hindrance to personal growth and happiness: the blind acceptance of traditional, conventional ways of living as handed down by previous generations. Too many individuals unquestioningly accept what their parents and grandparents believed to be the meaning of life; this is the root of man's present predicament. The narrator scoffs at the materialistic view of life that enjoys such popular currency. He advises his readers to embark on life as he has done, approaching it as a unique, personal experiment. No one should be tied down by society's definition of himself or life, but should confront life in a new, fresh way. By discarding those values of society which are worthless and sometimes dehumanizing, each individual would be able to discover life's meaning for himself. This is exactly what the narrator achieved by living at Walden, and it is what made possible his consequent spiritual growth as an individual.

The most dehumanizing of our traditional values, the narrator says, is the emphasis placed on property. To those smothered and enslaved by property, he offers the lesson he learned from critically evaluating his life: freedom to adventure upon the real concerns of life comes only after one has reduced his belongings to those things which are absolutely "necessary of life." While other men spent all of their time and energies piling up luxuries and maintaining their superabundant property, the narrator moved to Walden, reduced his needs to a bare minimum, and thus had the time and peace of mind to approach seriously the task of creating a fulfilling way of life. He knew that clothing, shelter, food, and fuel were the basic essentials for survival. And, unlike others, he did not slave his life away to acquire the latest clothing from Paris, a palatial estate, luxurious food, and costly fuel. He wore inexpensive but durable clothing. He borrowed an axe and built a simple, comfortable cabin for $28.12½, and kept his furniture to a minimum: a bed, a table, three chairs, cooking utensils, a lamp, and a desk. At first he kept a piece of limestone on his desk, but later he threw it away when he discovered how much time had to be spent in dusting it. He cultivated a small garden of beans, potatoes, corn, peas, and turnips which provided him with most of his food, and made a profit of $8.71½ by selling his surplus produce. He collected his fuel, free, from the woodside. What little extra money he needed, he earned from various day-labor jobs; he found that a man is able to support himself for a year with what he can earn in a few weeks. He advises his readers to follow his example by similarly simplifying their lives. Once out of the economic rat race, he said, they will have the leisure and tranquility to study, meditate, enjoy nature, and begin creating a spiritually rich life. Like the narrator, they will find that life can be a cause for celebration; life does not have to be a reason for weary complaint.

The narrator concludes this chapter by advising his readers *not* to go out and try to change the world once they have thrown off the fetters of tradition and materialism. The beginning of all real reform, he says, is the perfection of each individual. Once an individual has critically observed his shortcomings, his first step in reforming his life should be to turn inward, as the narrator did when he left society, and discover what he, alone, is capable of being. Within his self, he will discover a near-infinite potential for spiritual perfection which can be actualized. If, like the narrator, he designs his life to realize his potential for spiritual perfection, and avoids the world of trade which "curses every thing it handles," life will become a constantly growing state of ecstasy.

Commentary

Walden begins with the narrator's explanation of why he chose to address himself to his audience in the first person singular voice. "In most books, the *I*, or first person, is omitted; in this it will be retained; that, in respect to egotism, is the main difference. We commonly do not remember that it is, after all, always the first person that is speaking. I should not talk so much about myself if there were anybody else whom I knew as well." This declaration is immediately understandable in terms of Thoreau's strategy for his book. Thoreau desires *Walden* to have a forceful impact on society. His narrator will be explaining the rich changes in his life and how superior his life is when compared with that of the average American. He will explain how he achieved such a marvelous life, hoping to convince the reader to improve his own life. In doing this, he may become liable to the charge of hyperegotism or smugness. The narrator may be judged a braggart by the reader, and Thoreau counters this possibility by having his narrator immediately admit that his life is the subject at hand. Later the narrator almost deferentially tells his reader that "unfortunately, I am confined to this theme by the narrowness of my experience." Thus Thoreau further attempts to gain sympathy and a degree of empathy from the reader by creating a narrator who is almost reluctant to tell his unusual history.

There is, however, a more sophisticated level of meaning in the narrator's early comments about himself and his story. In emphasizing his use of the "I" voice, the narrator focuses the reader's attention on what is the primary subject of *Walden:* the subjective entity, the inner being, the self that will experience spiritual rebirth and growth at Walden Pond. Natural scenery, social criticism, economic and political theory—all of these have a prominent place in *Walden,* but all are subservient to the book's core: the quest to realize the "I" voice's vision of an ideal existence. The narrator moves through the objective, external world, but the real focus of the book is on the internal, subjective world of the narrator's self, or soul, as it moves toward spiritual fulfillment and ecstasy.

This movement toward spiritual perfection, the main movement of *Walden,* is expressed through metaphors. When the narrator starts to construct his cabin in March, 1845, he also, metaphorically, informs the reader that he is beginning to "build" a new self and a new life. As he proceeds, signs of rebirth and renewal suddenly appear. He tells us that "the ice in the pond was not yet dissolved," but as he works at his cabin ("builds" a new self), the iced pond (signifying his state of spiritual rigidity and lifelessness) continually thaws. The narrator makes clear this significant correspondence between the thawing ice and his own movement out of a spiritual "winter": "They were pleasant spring days, in which the winter of man's discontent was thawing itself as well as the earth, and the life that had lain torpid began to stretch itself." Nature "spring-ing" to life thus becomes a metaphorical expression of the new vitality the narrator was coming to feel. Next, he mentions a snake that ran into the pond and "lay on the bottom . . . more than a quarter of an hour; perhaps because he had not yet fairly come out of the torpid state" of winter hibernation. The narrator sees this half-awake snake as significant of his and other men's spiritual states. He finds hope for himself and others in considering that eventually the snake will be thawed by the sun; likewise, he and all men may be awakened from "their low and primitive condition" — if they allow themselves to feel the revivifying power of nature. He proclaims his belief that men "should feel the influence of the spring of springs arousing them"; if they do, he says, "they would of necessity rise to a higher and more ethereal life." The narrator is now moving toward this higher state of life, signaled by the song of "one early thrush." In Thoreau's writings, the songs of birds, particularly the thrush, are often used to symbolize inspiration.

Metaphors of rebirth are also used in the narrator's discussion of clothing and furniture. In criticizing man's obsession with fancy clothing and the fact that most people judge a man by his appearance rather than by the quality of his character, he indicates his own concern for the inner being that exists beneath the external shell. Man should first concern himself with the growth of inward perfection, since true beauty is born within the soul. To illustrate this, he turns to the natural phenomena of rebirth and renewal and points out that natural, true beauty must grow from within and cannot be externally applied: the "new" snake emerges from the old skin in the spring after having developed his new skin within the old; the caterpillar achieves its butterfly state by withdrawing and completing itself within its cocoon; and the loon renews its appearance by moulting, shedding its old feathers, and growing new ones. As animals transform themselves into more beautiful, more perfect creatures through internal growth, so must man concern himself with casting off the old, imperfect self and creating a new, more perfect one within if he is to become spiritually beautiful.

The subject of furniture provides the narrator with yet another opportunity to depict how he shed his old way of life for the sake of the new. Furniture, to the narrator, is like a "spider's web" which may entangle the "butterfly," Thoreau's symbol for the spiritually perfected man. Hence the narrator avoids collecting furniture — or rather, "sheds" it from his life. Alluding to the snake's sloughing-off process, he asks, "pray, for what do we *move* ever but to be rid of our furniture. . . ." Again making the same allusion to the snake's renewal, he praises the savages who annually go through the ritual of burning their belongings so as to start each year of their lives anew, unencumbered by property — "they at least go through the semblance of casting their slough annually." The narrator wishes that all men would "in like manner purify and prepare themselves" as he has done. He has cast off furniture, tradition, debts, and the worries of an ordinary, materialistic life. He has cast off his old *social* personality for the sake of developing a new, more perfect soul.

The preponderant number of metaphors associated with purification, rebirth, and renewal leads the reader to conclude that the "I" voice's main concern, and *Walden's* most important theme, deals with the possibility of transcending one's old life and being reborn into a spiritually elevated one.

CHAPTER TWO

Where I Lived, and What I Lived For

Summary

The narrator tells us that for many years he thought of buying a farm in the Concord countryside. He considered many sites and even exercised his Yankee shrewdness by haggling over the price with several farmers. But he followed his own advice, as expressed in "Economy," and avoided purchasing a farm because it would inevitably tie him down financially and complicate his life. Besides, he reasoned, why did he need to *own* a farm? All that is of real value to the individual in living on a farm — close, personal contact with the spiritually invigorating influences of nature — can be had for nothing.

The Hollowell place did, however, offer a special advantage that the narrator desired: "its complete retirement, being about two miles from the village, half a mile from the nearest neighbour, and separated from the highway." He desired solitude, but not the Hollowell mortgage, so he created a suitable substitute — a primitive, inexpense "farm" on the shore of Walden. He declared his own independence from society and mortgages on July 4, 1845, by moving into his pond-side hut. There he found himself free from the trivialities of village life, free from the economic rat race, and free to be inspired by nature.

He relates the spiritual ecstasy that came to him immediately after moving to Walden. He was so content, so totally happy while enjoying the ripeness of summer and the songs of various birds that he came to see his new residence as no longer a simple hut but as a "new and unprofaned part of the universe." To some, it might have seemed a poor excuse for a house, but to the inspired narrator it had a divine character.

The narrator especially enjoyed his mornings at Walden. He found each one to be "a cheerful invitation to make my life of equal simplicity, and I may say innocence, with Nature herself." As he bathed in the pond, he was both physically and spiritually invigorated; he realized that he was truly awakening to not only the day, but to life itself.

Having provided an example of how his life became fresh and vitally alive, the narrator turns to his readers and asks why they continue to live as drably as they do. He wonders why men persist in living "meanly, like ants" when life *can be* a joyful celebration. He complains that "our life is frittered away by detail," and that most men's personalities are uncomfortably split into many opposing parts. Holding up his own example of spiritual wholeness, he offers his readers the remedy for spiritual disintegration that he discovered and announced in "Economy": "Simplicity, simplicity, simplicity! I say, let your affairs be as two or three, and not a hundred or a thousand. . . . Simplify, simplify." Moreover, he declares that we should push aside all of the trivialities of life and immediately get down to the real, genuine concerns of life. For example, we should quit wasting our time reading the worthless, repetitive gossip that fills the daily newspapers and seek out the real truths of existence.

The narrator was able to do this, and we watch him as he continues his "burrowing" toward truth; "I would mine and burrow my way through these hills. I think that the richest vein is somewhere hereabouts." As *Walden* progresses, we shall see the spiritual riches that he "mined" from living at Walden Pond.

Commentary

In considering this chapter, the first thing the reader should note is the similarity between the image of the narrator at the beginning of the chapter and that at the end. At the beginning, he described the poet—himself—who had the ability to "skim off" from the landscape that which was of value to his soul. He did not buy the Hollowell farm, but he did retain in his mind the landscape; "and I have since annually carried off what it yielded without a wheelbarrow." At the end of the chapter, we find him "mining" reality, digging out of life those values that make him complete. Throughout *Walden*, we will see the narrator acting thus: approaching books, animals, sounds, and all the aspects of life in terms of their value to his process of self-growth. In effect, anything in the world exists for the sake of what it can contribute to his quest for perfection. As he states midway in this chapter, "I wanted to live deep and suck out all the marrow of life."

This chapter dramatically illustrates the success of the narrator's attempt at "mining," "skimming off," and "sucking out" that which is of spiritual value. As in "Economy," the narrator's growing state of inspiration is signaled by the songs of birds; again Thoreau's special symbol of inspiration appears as "the wood thrush sang around, and was heard from shore to shore." As the narrator bathes in the pond, we discover still other symbols of spiritual purification, that of water and the religious ceremony of baptism. The narrator is careful to make this allusion clear: "I got up early and bathed in the pond; that was a religious exercise, and one of the best things which I did." That this symbolic action takes place in the morning is also significant. As the new day is born, the narrator believes that with each dawn a new life begins for him: "Morning is when I am awake and there is a dawn in me." The narrator believes that he daily moves further out of the spiritually asleep state that he once shared with the majority of men, the "sleepers." He is no longer like the half-thawed snake of "Economy" that slumbered on the bottom of Walden Pond.

At the conclusion of "Economy," the narrator announced that the first step to personal reform is the act of turning inward to discover one's potential for greatness. As this chapter indicates, one thing that the narrator found within himself was the faculty of imagination which enabled him to see himself and the world in a new, more spiritually perfect way—hence his discovery that his hut near the pond was actually a palace, in terms of its value to the development of his spiritual life. The most noteworthy imaginative act that the narrator performs is to create a new definition of his relationship to the world. When he declares, "Wherever I sat, there might I live, and the landscape radiated from me accordingly," he is making a declaration of independence even more significant than his act of moving to the pond. He is reversing a view of man's nature which had enjoyed currency for centuries. The narrator rejects the old, specifically the eighteenth-century, vision of man's relation to the universe. For centuries, the popular idea of this relationship was that an individual was supposed to fit into his preordained place, or "slot," in the world—that is, conform to a pre-established plan for his role in life. Theoretically, this "slot" was assigned by God, who had arranged a tight order in the universe in which all forms of existence had a definite place. Practically speaking, the individual's "slot," then as now, was determined by tradition and authority. The narrator dramatically reverses this scheme by announcing that he, his consciousness, is the center of the universe. He will not fit into the world; rather, the world will fit around him. He will not exist in relation to the world; because he is the center of all existence, the world will exist in relation to him. He chooses not to fit into a particular place in life and be limited to it — which would have occurred if he had bought the Hollowell farm; instead of having his life ordered for him by the routine of farm life or the laws of society, he will give *his* order to his life and to the world around him. In effect, he is creating not only a new inner self, but also a new world as well, *his* world. By placing himself at the center of his universe, he once again emphasizes the primary significance of the "I" voice of *Walden;* again the reader's attention is directed to the subjective entity in the process of moving toward perfection.

CHAPTER THREE

Reading

Summary

In "Economy," the narrator advised his readers to cast off the inessential baggage of civilization so as to be free to adventure upon the great experiment of living. Great books, however, are one of the inheritances that men should not discard. While most of what men inherit from previous generations — conventions, property, and money — is antithetical to spiritual growth, "books are the treasured wealth of the world and the fit inheritance of generations and nations." The narrator speaks from experience on this point; and while he does not read much at Walden, he realizes the value of literature in his attempt at spiritual growth. He believes that "in dealing with truth we are immortal." The permanent, fixed expression of truth available in literature is thus an absolute necessity for the individual in quest of transcendence. He has found the writings of Homer and Aeschylus to be of greatest value, "for what are the classics but the noblest recorded thoughts of man?" By reading Dante, Shakespeare, and Oriental and Western scriptures, "we may hope to scale heaven at last."

Having talked about the value of reading great literature, the narrator turns next to the spiritual "sleepers" of society and chides them for their unwillingness to profit from reading and their lamentable eagerness to read shallow, popular fiction. He complains that most men "vegetate and dissipate their faculties in what is called easy reading." The narrator gives a description of this easy reading which accurately characterizes the bulk of popular fiction in nineteenth-century America. To the narrator, it is no wonder that men, and their society, are so spiritually dead. Shabby literature can create only shabby minds.

The narrator concludes the chapter by indicting society for not providing a culture which would awaken the "sleepers." In Concord, and in America, he finds a culture "worthy only of pigmies and manikins. . . . we soar but little higher [than small birds] in our intellectual flights." He calls for a new society dedicated not only to trade and agriculture, but to human culture. Society should be the patron of the fine arts and act to establish "uncommon schools" so that men might discover the real significance of life. We should make our villages into centers of culture so that we might one day have "noble villages of men."

Commentary

That the narrator does not read much while at Walden will be seen as significant if the reader recalls Emerson's three-part description of the transcendentalist's activities: he enriches himself with the wisdom of the past; he is ennobled by the experience of nature; and he attempts to renovate society. Apparently the narrator has already fulfilled the first requisite of the transcendental life and has "skimmed off" much of what is valuable to his life from the literature of the past. This chapter constitutes a description of what the narrator has gained from reading and an exhortation that the reader "mine" the same vein of spiritual truth.

That literature has proven to be a very rich vein for the narrator is indicated by his repeated use of the "new day" metaphor, which indicates spiritual awakening and rebirth. He tells us that the classics are "as beautiful almost as the morning itself," and that he devotes his "most alert and wakeful hours" to the reading of them. He advises his readers to "consecrate morning hours" to Homer and Aeschylus, and promises that spiritual rejuvenation will result: "How many a man has dated a new era in his life from the reading of a book." Images quite the opposite of rebirth are associated with the easy reading of the "sleepers": "The result is dulness of sight, a stagnation of the vital circulations, and a general deliquium."

The reader should especially note the narrator's call for social reform at the end of the chapter. This image of the narrator as a man with a real sense of social concern is one that critics of Thoreau usually manage to overlook when they term him an anti-social recluse.

CHAPTER FOUR

Sounds

Summary

The narrator begins this chapter by cautioning the reader against an overreliance on literature as a means to transcendence. While it does offer an avenue to truth, literature is the expression of an author's experience of reality and should not be used as a substitute for reality itself. We should immediately experience the richness of life at first hand if we desire spiritual elevation; thus we see the great significance of the narrator's admission that "I did not read books the first summer; I hoed beans."

The narrator is telling us that he directly experienced nature at the pond, and he felt ecstatic as he sat in the doorway of his hut, enjoying the beauty of a summer morning "while the birds sang around or flitted noiseless through the house." He succinctly depicts his happy state thus: "I silently smiled at my incessant good fortune." He was unperturbed by the thought that his spiritually sleeping townsmen would, no doubt, criticize his situation as one of sheer idleness; they, however, did not know the delights that they were missing.

The narrator's revery is interrupted by the rattle of railroad cars and a locomotive's shrill whistle. He attempts to retain his

...ery by contemplating upon the railroad's value to man ...admirable sense of American enterprise and industry ...it represents. But the longer he considers it, the more irritated he becomes, and his ecstasy departs. He realizes that the whistle announces the demise of the pastoral, agrarian way of life—the life he enjoys most—and the rise of industrial America, with its factories, sweatshops, crowded urban centers, and assembly lines. The easy, natural, poetic life, as typified by his idyllic life at Walden, is being displaced; he recognizes the railroad as a kind of enemy. The narrator declares that he will avoid it: "I will not have my eyes put out and my ears spoiled by its smoke, and steam, and hissing."

Once the train passes, the narrator's ecstasy returns. Listening to the bells of distant towns, to the lowing of cows in a pasture beyond the woods, and the songs of whippoorwills, his sense of wholeness and fulfillment grows as his day moves into evening. But, with the night, a new type of sound is heard, the "most solemn graveyard ditty" of owls. To the narrator, this is the "dark and tearful side of music." He interprets the owls' notes to reflect "the stark twilight and unsatisfied thoughts which all have," but he is not depressed. He knows that nature's song of hope and rebirth, the jubilant cry of the cock at dawn, will surely follow the despondent notes of the owls. This gives support to his optimistic faith that all melancholy is short-lived and must eventually give way to hope and fulfillment when one lives close to nature.

Commentary

While the chapter does deal with the ecstasy produced in the narrator by various sounds, the title has a broader significance. Thoreau is stressing the primary value of immediate, sensual experience; to live the transcendental life, one must not only read and think about life but experience it directly.

As the chapter opens, we find the narrator doing just that. He is awake to life and is "forever on the alert," "looking always at what is to be seen" in his surroundings. Thus he opens himself to the stimulation of nature. The result, by now, is predictable, and the reader should note the key metaphors of rebirth (summer morning, bath, sunrise, birds singing). The fact that he spiritually "grew in those seasons like corn in the night" is symbolized by an image of nature's spring rebirth: "The large buds, suddenly pushing out late in the spring from dry sticks which had seemed to be dead, developed themselves as by magic into graceful green and tender boughs." Like nature, he has come from a kind of spiritual death to life and now toward fulfillment.

The locomotive's interruption of the narrator's revery is one of the most noteworthy incidents in *Walden*. It is very significant that it is an unnatural, mechanical sound that intrudes upon his revery and jerks him back to the progressive, mechanical reality of the nineteenth century, the industrial revolution, the growth of trade, and the death of agrarian culture. It is interesting to observe the narrator's reaction to this intrusion. He is an individual who is striving for a natural, integrated self, an integrated vision of life, and before him are two clashing images, depicting two antithetical worlds: lush, sympathetic nature, and the cold, noisy, unnatural, inhuman machine. He has criticized his townsmen for living fractured lives and living in a world made up of opposing, irreconcilable parts, yet now the machine has clanged and whistled its way into his tranquil world of natural harmony; now he finds himself open to the same criticism of disintegration. Being one who is always "looking at what is to be seen," he cannot ignore these jarring images. So, he attempts to use the power within—that is, imagination—to transform the machine into a part of nature. If this works, he will again have a wholesome, integrated vision of reality, and then he may recapture his sense of spiritual wholeness. Therefore, he imaginatively applies natural imagery to the train: the rattling cars sound "like the beat of a partridge." Once again he uses a natural simile to make the train a part of the fabric of nature: "the whistle of the locomotive penetrates my woods summer and winter, sounding like the scream of a hawk sailing over some farmer's yard." Having thus engaged his poetic faculties to transform the unnatural into the natural, he continues along this line of thought, moving past the simple level of simile to the more complex level of myth. And his mythological treatment of the train provides him with a cause for optimism about man's condition: "When I hear the iron horse make the hills echo with his snort-like thunder, shaking the earth with his feet, and breathing fire and smoke from his nostrils . . . it seems as if the earth had got a race now worthy to inhabit it."

Since, for the transcendentalist, myths as well as nature reveal truths about man, the narrator "skims off" the spiritual significance of this train-creature he has imaginatively created. In this product of the industrial revolution, he is able to find a symbol of the Yankee virtues of perserverance and fortitude necessary for the man who would achieve transcendence. In the locomotive, man has "constructed a fate, an *Atropos*, that never turns aside." By advising his readers to "let that be the name of your engine," the narrator reveals that he admires the steadfastness and high purposefulness represented by the locomotive. The train is also a symbol for the world of commerce; and since commerce "is very natural in its methods, withal," the narrator derives truths for men from it. He finds represented in commerce the heroic, self-reliant spirit necessary for maintaining the transcendental quest: "What recommends commerce to me is its enterprise and bravery. It does not clasp its hands and pray to Jupiter." It also illustrates other qualities of the elevated man: "Commerce is unexpectedly confident and serene, alert, adventurous, and unwearied."

All of this sounds fine, and it would seem that the narrator has succeeded in integrating the machine world into his world; it would seem that he could now resume his ecstasy at an even higher level because of his great imaginative triumph. But our narrator is not an idealistic fool. He prides himself on his hardheaded realism, and while he mythically and poetically views the railroad and the commercial world, his critical judgment is still operative. When he declares that "it seems as if the earth had got a race now worthy to inhabit it." he simultaneously deflates his myth by piercing through the appearance, the "seems," of his poetic vision and complaining, "if all were as it seems, and men made the elements their servants for noble ends!" Of course, the railroad and commerce, in general, are not serving noble ends. The railroad is serving commerce and commerce is serving itself; and despite the enterprise and bravery of the whole adventure, the railroad tracks lead back to the world of economic drudgery, to the world of the "sleepers." The locomotive has stimulated the production of more quantities for the consumer, but it has not substantially improved the spiritual quality of life. According to the narrator, the locomotive and the industrial revolution that spawned it have cheapened life. The industrialization of America has destroyed the old, agrarian way of life that the narrator prefers; it has abruptly displaced those who lived it.

As a car-load of sheep rattle by, he sadly views "a car-load of drovers, too, in the midst, on a level with their droves now, their vocation gone, but still clinging to their useless sticks as their badge of office." They are the first victims of automation in its infancy. The narrator then suddenly realizes that he too is a potential victim. In moving to Walden and by farming, he adopted the pastoral way of life — of which the shepherd, or drover, is a traditional symbol. Seeing the drovers displaced by the railroad, he realizes that "so is your pastoral life whirled past and away." It is only when the train is gone that the narrator is able to resume his revery. But it should be noted that this problem has not been solved.

The narrator concludes the chapter with a symbol of the degree to which nature has fulfilled him. Having passed the melancholy night, with its songs of sadness sung by owls, he finds his sense of spiritual vitality and hope unimpaired. We are symbolically informed of his continuing ecstasy when he describes "unfenced Nature reaching up to your very [window] sills." The wild, overflowing abundance of life in nature reflects — as it did in the beginning of this chapter — the narrator's spiritual vitality and "ripeness."

CHAPTER FIVE

Solitude

Summary

As the chapter opens, we find the narrator has seemingly forgotten the railroad incident and is once again in ecstasy. He feels so much in harmony with nature that he declares that he is "a part of herself." The evening is so "delicious" and his sense of oneness with nature so great, that he can barely express himself: "Sympathy with the fluttering alder and poplar leaves almost takes my breath." His belief that the melancholy thoughts stirred by the owls' notes would eventually give way to happiness is confirmed. His present bliss proves that "there can be no very black melancholy to him who lives in the midst of Nature, and has his senses still." At this moment of spiritual fulfillment, when "every little pine needle expanded and swelled with sympathy, and befriended me," the narrator recalls an ironic statement of his townsmen: "I should think you would feel lonesome down there, and want to be nearer to folks, rainy and snowy days and nights especially."

Having been fulfilled by the "sweet and tender" society of nature, the narrator finds this statement to be almost laughable. Since nature offers a contentment not to be found in the human society which the townsmen think so important, he feels justified in giving a sharp response to this idea. What is the sense in living next to the depot, the barroom, the meeting house, or the grocery? What great value is there in rubbing elbows with other men? He has found that "society is commonly too cheap. We meet at very short intervals, not having had time to acquire any new value for each other. We meet at meals three times a day, and give each other a new taste of that old musty cheese that we are." As the willow sends its roots in the direction of nourishment, so does the spiritually minded narrator; and his spiritual nourishment is not to be found in Concord, but in the "perennial source of life," nature.

In the gentle, benevolent, revitalizing company of nature, loneliness is an irrelevant concern. He feels so much a part of nature that to ask him if he is lonely is like asking the loon in the pond, a January thaw, the north star, or Walden Pond itself if they are lonely.

Commentary

If the reader wonders how the narrator finds the "company" of nature superior to human company, he should consider

Thoreau's view of nature. Thoreau saw it as both a tremendous source of sensual pleasure, capable of revitalizing the physical man in him, and as the medium through which the spiritual world might be experienced. To him, it was literally a "perennial source of life," physical and spiritual. To be in harmony with nature meant to be physically and spiritually whole. Thoreau seemed to find human company incapable of stimulating him to such a feeling of wholeness; hence, it was judged inferior to nature.

The stimulation received from a solitary relationship with nature is described with metaphors of rebirth and renewal. The narrator claims that he was no more lonely than a loon (he undergoes an annual moulting, a sign of renewal) or a January thaw (signifying movement out of a wintry, lifeless spiritual state). We should note the pun when the narrator significantly states, "I find it *wholesome* to be alone."

When the narrator states that he is no more lonely than Walden Pond, he introduces a new metaphoric sequence of *Walden*. The pond is later developed as a metaphor for the narrator's purified and perfected soul.

CHAPTER SIX

Visitors

Summary

"I am naturally no hermit," begins the narrator, "I think that I love society as much as most." Although much of his time at Walden was spent in solitary communion with nature, he did from time to time entertain visitors. In fact, he once had twenty-five people under his roof at one time. Yet, for the most part, the distance from Concord so cut down on the number of interruptions to his solitary life that he usually met only people worth meeting: "Fewer came to see me on trivial business. . . . I had withdrawn so far within the great ocean of solitude, into which the rivers of society empty, that for the most part, so far as my needs were concerned, only the finest sediment was deposited around me."

One of the narrator's favorite visitors was a Canadian woodchopper. He delighted in the company of the woodchopper because of his simple, honest personality—"a more simple and
natural man it would be hard to find." To the narrator, the woodchopper led a perfect life; that is, rose early, was free from
anxiety, and was liberated from economic drudgery because he
lived on the level of mere subsistence, close to nature. He was
such a "natural" person that birds perched on his shoulders as
he ate his lunch. The narrator—still "skimming off" truths—
was ready to declare him the ideal man, but then he noted a sub-
stantial defect. The woodchopper was content in nature, but
content mainly in the sense that a well-fed ox is. "The intellectual and what is called spiritual man in him were slumbering as in
an infant." The woodchopper was natural and did not suffer from
the artificiality of society, yet he, like the townsmen, was a
"sleeper."

There were other visitors. Half-witted men from the alms-
house stopped by, and the narrator was not too surprised to find
"some of them to be wiser than the so-called *overseers* of the
poor and selectmen of the town." "Restless, committed men"
also came to the pond but did not enjoy themselves. They had
been so spiritually enervated by the economic world that they
could not feel the benign influences of nature. "The greatest
bores of all," social reformers—men who go about trying to
change the world without having first reformed themselves—
came to preach at the narrator; he avoided these distasteful
"men-harriers." The only visitors who truly seemed to enjoy
their trek to the pond were those who had not yet been ruined by
society, young girls and boys. "They looked in the pond at the
flowers, and improved their time." The narrator is delighted
that there are still such people—"for I had had communication
with that race."

Commentary

The narrator's claim that he loves society as much as most
is not a very convincing one, even though he qualifies this statement later in the chapter. When he declares that he "might

possibly sit out the sturdiest frequenter of the barroom, if my business called me thither," it is difficult to know if the narrator is serious; perhaps he is indulging in humor, perhaps self-parody. Despite his claims to the contrary, the narrator is not really a "society-loving" man; we need consider only how few visitors he enthusiastically describes to realize how much more he prefers solitude in nature to society. If the narrator seems to be straining to prove he is sociable, it is because of the author's intent for his book. Thoreau desires it to have a strong impact on society; to do this, he must create an attractive narrator. Hence Thoreau attempts to make him a more "regular" fellow by downplaying his preference for solitude.

That the narrator was not too inspired by visitors may be most clearly seen when we recall how many metaphors of rebirth appeared in the previous chapter; in "Visitors," there are none. Harmony with nature and ecstasy seemingly cease when the narrator greets visitors from town.

CHAPTER SEVEN

The Bean-field

Summary

A principle activity of the narrator was tending his bean-field. It was a large one, "the length of whose rows, added together, was seven miles," and it provided him with food and a source of cash — beans and other vegetables gave him a profit of $8.71½. Early each morning he attacked the weeds with his hoe, examined the arrowheads and bits of pottery he turned up, and — most important of all — *enjoyed* his work. For it was more than just work; it was an opportunity to experience prolonged close contact with nature. Here was yet another chance to enjoy life to the fullest, and the narrator sharply criticizes those farmers who till the soil only for a financial gain. The narrator recalls that "husbandry was once a sacred art," an activity of genuine spiritual value. His is, and will continue to be, a more valuable crop than that which fills barns. His experience has taught him that the "true husbandman," the man who approaches nature with a spiritual harvest in mind, "will cease from anxiety." Fulfillment, contentment, and tranquility are the real produce that the narrator reaped from his bean-field.

Commentary

In the previous chapter, the narrator was finally not able to accept the way of life that the woodchopper represented. He admired the woodchopper's close ties with nature, but he saw it as a limitation that the woodchopper lacked the intellect, intuition, and imagination necessary for complete transcendence. The narrator wished to live a spiritual life, but he also wanted it to be a natural life—one that was intimate with earth, as well as with heaven. And thus we come to the profound value of growing beans: "They attached me to the earth, and so I got strength like Antaeus." (Antaeus was the son of the goddess of the earth and derived his strength from contact with his mother; Hercules could defeat him in battle only by lifting him from the ground, thereby cutting off the source of his energy.) This is one value that the narrator derived from working in his bean-field, and there are others. One is that his method of raising beans enabled him to establish a way of life in a state between wild, untamed nature and well-ordered civilization; in this way, he was able to derive what was of value to him from both worlds. From the world of man, he derived his occupation: cultivating the soil. But he attempted to remain as natural as possible by not manuring his fields or using any farm implements except a hoe. The parable is obvious enough. When the narrator says of his bean-field, "mine was, as it were, the connecting link between wild and cultivated fields," he is claiming that he was civilized to a degree short of the excessive artificiality and unnaturalness of society, and he was natural to a degree short of uncultivated, untamed wilderness. He sees himself, then, as a symbol of humanized nature and naturalized civilization. He has forged in his personality a link between two worlds and is able to enjoy the best of both worlds.

The reader should note above that the bean-field has been interpreted to signify the narrator's inner state. The bean-field remains a literal bean-field and a source of physical stimulation to the narrator, but it is also a metaphor for the narrator's self—a self that needs the simultaneous experience of nature and spirit, and of wildness and civilization. In the chapter entitled "Where I Lived, and What I Lived For," the narrator parenthetically mentioned, "I have always cultivated a garden," the garden being a metaphor for his self. And at the beginning of "The Bean-field," he attempts to prod the reader into considering this significance of his "garden." He indicates that there is a deeper meaning to his bean-field by asking, "what was the meaning of this," "why should I raise them," and "what shall I learn of beans or beans of me?" That the bean-field has a spiritual significance is suggested offhandedly by his answer: "only Heaven knows." The narrator has come to Walden Pond to cultivate and improve himself and, with this in mind, we might profitably read his description of how he cultivated the "soil": "This was my curious labour all summer—to make this portion of the earth's surface, which had yielded only cinquefoil, blackberries, john-swort, and the like, before, sweet wild fruits and pleasant flowers, produce instead this pulse." With the narrator's process of inner development and perfection in mind, we can see the metaphorical significance of his assertion that cultivating a garden was his "day's work" in this "summer" of spiritual growth. As a cultivated garden gives birth to beans instead of weeds, the narrator's soul will develop finer attributes because of his efforts at self-culture. He is an artist creating, like a sculptor with his clay, a soul, making his self express its spiritual perfection.

As would be expected, such a deliberate and successful cultivation of self enables the narrator to experience ecstasy. The metaphors of summer, morning, and dew (a metaphor expressing the freshness of morning) have already indicated this, but other metaphors of inspiration are also presented. As he worked his field, the narrator remembers that "near at hand, upon the top-most spray of a birch, [sang] the brown-thrasher—or red mavis, as some love to call him—all the morning." He remembers looking up to the sky and seeing a nighthawk circling his cabin. And he makes the inspirational significance of hawks clear when he describes "a pair of hen-hawks circling high in the sky, alternately soaring and descending, approaching and leaving one another, as if they were the embodiment of my own thoughts." Like the hawks, the narrator is also "high" (ecstastic) — because of the delight he receives from cultivating his "garden."

The intense degree of this ecstasy is indicated by the following statement: "When my hoe tinkled against the stones, that music echoed to the woods and the sky, and was an accompaniment to my labour which yielded an instant and immeasurable crop. It was no longer beans that I hoed, nor I that hoed beans." The "crop" that the narrator harvests is total, immediate, ecstatic integration with nature, and thus the divine. It is a nirvana-like state that he experiences; he is no longer distinct from nature or spirit: all is One. It is no longer beans (an object apart from himself) that he hoes, or an "I" (an entity apart from beans) that hoes the beans. All individuality disappears in this mystical fusion with nature and the divine.

CHAPTER EIGHT

The Village

Summary

After hoeing, reading, or writing in the forenoon the narrator bathed, and "every day or two," strolled to Concord to hear the latest news. He found that the news of the town, "was really as refreshing in its way as the rustle of the leaves." Unfortunately, the townsmen did not share his view of how a bit of news now and then can be refreshing. When he arrived in town, he found the people numbed by their addiction to the news. Walking down a main street, he observed that it was lined by bored men longing for the latest news.

The narrator was especially upset by the intense stares of these news-hungry villagers. He was even more disturbed by the advertising which seemed to try and draw him back into the materialistic life. The narrator resisted these lures by keeping his mind on "high things" as he proceeded down the street.

Once back in the woods, the narrator found it easier to think about "high things." When considering how people often lose their way in the woods on dark nights, he came upon a transcendental truth: "Not till we are completely lost, or turned around—for a man needs only to be turned round once with his eyes shut in this world to be lost—do we appreciate the vastness and strangeness of Nature." Transcendence depends upon creating a new vision of reality and one's relationship to it. To create a new life depends upon seeing a new world, as though one were "lost" and seeing a world never known before.

A chief obstacle to creating a new vision of life is the state and the society that supports it. The narrator moved to Walden Pond to create a new life, a *personal* life which would be vastly different from that proposed by society and enforced by the laws of the state. He did not wish to conform to the will of the majority; yet, he found that "wherever a man goes, men will pursue him and paw him with their dirty institutions, and, if they can, constrain him to belong to their desperate odd-fellow society." To illustrate this point, he tells how one day he was arrested because he did not pay his tax to a "state which buys and sells men, women, and children, like cattle at the door of its senate-house." Human slavery is not a part of his new vision of life, and he deeply resents the state's forcible attempt to make it a part of that vision. In fact, a government should not force anyone to do or believe anything. If a government feels obliged to try and guide men, it should do so by good example alone: "You who govern public affairs, what need have you to employ punishments? Love virtue, and the people will be virtuous."

Commentary

Thoreau's sense of humor comes into play in this chapter as it did in "Visitors." There he began by overstating the narrator's love of society and then proceeded to show how little he relished society. Here the narrator begins by declaring how refreshing a visit to the town can be; then he spends the rest of the chapter describing how irritating such a visit actually is. Picture the narrator walking down the street, with the eyes of the curious

46

townfolk upon him; then consider what he says: "Sometimes I bolted suddenly, and nobody could tell my whereabouts."

The reader will once again note that this chapter began with the narrator's bathing. If this metaphor of purification seems belabored by now, it is because Thoreau is making sure that the reader realizes the deep significance of Walden Pond's purity — a point which is stressed in the next chapter. The pond, remember, is a metaphor for the narrator's purified soul.

CHAPTER NINE

The Ponds

Summary

Having returned to the woods and resumed his solitary, tranquil life, the narrator spent most of his time being continually "refreshed" by rambling about the surrounding countryside. He climbed Fair-Haven Hill and enjoyed the "ambrosial" flavors of ripe huckleberries and blueberries. Occasionally, after his hoeing was done for the day, he went fishing, sometimes with an elderly fisherman who also enjoyed the pond. On warm evenings, the narrator simply drifted about in his boat, playing his flute and observing the perch circling below him. Thus he spent his days and nights, enjoying a kind of idyllic contentment and ease.

The narrator turns next to the center of all of this happy activity, Walden Pond, and gives a minute description of it which comprises most of the chapter. Then he describes the other bodies of water in the Concord area: Flint's Pond, Goose Pond, White Pond, and Fair-Haven Bay.

Commentary

"The Ponds" can best be described as a cluster of metaphors which is designed to illuminate Thoreau's concept of the ideal self, or soul. He focuses the reader's attention on the self of the narrator by presenting a situation which the reader should find familiar. It is a *dialectical situation* — meaning that the narrator's self confronts two apparently opposite aspects of life which must be brought together — that is, *synthesized* or *integrated*. The narrator has presented such a situation three times previously: in "Sounds," he had to overcome the conflict between the world of Nature and the world of the Machine, represented by the noisy train; in "The Bean-field," he brought together, and made one, the world of Nature and the world of Civilization; and in "Visitors," he introduced through the character of the woodchopper a conflict which also begins this chapter. It will be recalled that the woodchopper was admirable because of his naturalness, yet he was not ideal because he lacked spiritual awareness. The narrator wants both of these qualities in his life; his self, he believes, should be both natural and spiritual (*super*natural). He wants to bring together these two apparently opposite worlds of nature and spirit within his self.

At the beginning of "The Ponds," the narrator metaphorically informs us that he has made this synthesis within his self. He tells us that while fishing at night he felt this integration take place: "It was very queer, especially in dark nights, when your thoughts had wandered to vast and cosmogonal themes in other spheres, to feel this faint jerk, which came to interrupt your dreams and link you to Nature again. It seemed as if I might next cast my line upward into the air, as well as downward into this element which was scarcely more dense. Thus I caught two fishes, as it were, with one hook." He has his "lines" connected to the worlds of Nature and Spirit; his self has integrated the two. And note the locale at which the two "lines" meet: Walden Pond — the metaphor for the narrator's now integrated, now fulfilled self. Later, in a bit of verse, the narrator again indicates this metaphorical identification between his perfected self and Walden Pond: "I am its stony shore/ . . . And its deepest resort/ Lies high in my thought." At another point, he reemphasizes the fact that his soul, partaking of Nature and Spirit, is signified by a pond that is "intermediate in its nature between the land and sky."

With this metaphorical relationship in mind, we may proceed to a profitable reading of the narrator's description of the pond. There are four main ways in which the narrator describes the pond, and thus metaphorically describes his perfected soul.

1. *The purity of Walden Pond:* There have been abundant metaphors of purification presented up to this point in *Walden.* Thus far we have seen the narrator abstaining from luxurious foods and ascetically choosing his meals. He avoids meat and other foods of a "non-spiritual" nature. Like the snake, he has purified himself by sloughing off his old life and the corrupting influences of society. His attempt at purifying his spirit has also been repeatedly emphasized by the number of times he bathes. Hence it is not surprising that the pond is "so remarkable for its depth and purity." Repeatedly, he makes this point: "it is a clear and deep green well"; "this water is of such crystalline purity"; "the water is so transparent"; "the bottom is pure sand"; "it is pure at all times"; and "all the fishes which inhabit this pond are much cleaner, handsomer, and firmer fleshed than those in the river and most other ponds, as the water is purer."

2. *Its divine nature:* Previously we have discussed how nature is the medium through which the divine expresses itself to man. We have also discussed the view of man's self being divine once spiritual elevation is accomplished. Accordingly, we see the pond metaphor expressing the idea of divinity in two ways: as the medium of divine expression and as the metaphor which expresses the divinity of the narrator's self. We find that the pond has "obtained a patent of heaven to be the only Walden Pond in the world and distiller of celestial dews." It is "sky water," "God's Drop," and being sacred, by definition, it is not profane: "I doubt if it is ever profaned by the wing of a gull, like Fair-Haven." While thinking about his visits to Walden during his youth, the narrator concludes that it has never changed its divine character: "The same thought is welling up to its surface that was then; it is the same liquid joy and happiness to itself and its Maker, ay, and it *may* be to me. It is the work of a brave man surely, in whom there was no guile! He rounded this water with his hand, deepened and clarified it in his thought, and in his will bequeathed it to Concord." The narrator thus explains through the pond metaphor that his self is the expression of the

divine mind and that his highest thoughts are divine in nature, "deepened and clarified" by the mind of God.

3. *A metaphor for inspiration:* The term "inspiration" literally denotes the flow of spirit into an individual's soul, the result being a heightened intellectual and emotional state. With this in mind, we may comprehend the description of the pond as his inspired self. He significantly declares that "a field of water betrays the spirit that is in the air. It is continually receiving new life and motion from above." Inspiration has been traditionally described with the figure of an overflowing spring, and several times in this chapter the narrator focuses on "where a spring welled up from the bottom." To further emphasize the inspirational character of Walden, the narrator frequently reiterates that "Walden has no visible inlet or outlet"; as the narrator well knows, no one can objectively describe the exact way in which one receives inspiration. But the narrator does, through the pond metaphor, depict how inspiration comes and goes in himself. We have frequently seen the narrator in intense states of inspiration. But his ecstasy has not been constant; it varies from time to time. Thus, over and over, the narrator refers to the inconstant level of the pond's depth: "it had commenced to rise and fall"; "the pond rises and falls"; and "this rise and fall of Walden."

4. *The eye-spiritual vision metaphor.* Early in his description of the pond, while discussing the color of Walden's water, the narrator states: "It may be simply the result of the prevailing blue mixed with the yellow of the sand. Such is the colour of its iris." With the term "iris," he introduces the metaphor of the eye. The eye metaphor is later developed more fully when the narrator declares: "It is the earth's eye, looking into which the beholder measures the depth of his own nature." And the narrator does look into it. Repeatedly, we find him "looking directly down into our waters from a boat." The choice of the words "our waters" is appropriate, for here we have the narrator metaphorically turning inward and viewing his self. Note that this self that the narrator looks into is portrayed as an eye which looks toward heaven. What Thoreau is depicting is the conscious mind (one kind of "eye" or vision) looking into the deepest self, the

unconscious, the self that intuitively knows, or "sees," God (it is the other kind of "eye"; non-rational, spiritual vision). Thus the narrator indicates his awareness of a faculty for spiritual vision within himself; he is claiming that within himself is an ability to perceive the divine. And it is interesting to note that the narrator, who is peering into the "pond," is within the range of vision of this metaphorical "eye"; the eye that perceives the divine perceives him. Here is still another example of the divine nature of the narrator's self.

There are many other angles from which the pond is metaphorically viewed as the narrator's self. It expresses rejuvenation: "it is perennially young." It reveals the narrator's typical emotional state: "the constant welling-up of its fountain, the gentle pulsing of its life, the heaving of its breast." It represents pre-Adamic innocence: "Perhaps on that spring morning when Adam and Eve were driven out of Eden, Walden Pond was already in existence" and perhaps it "had not heard of the fall," thus remaining uncorrupted by "original sin." When we listen to the narrator describe the profound depths of Walden, we may recall that he spoke earlier of man's nature as being of an infinite extent. Thus, through these several metaphors, we are told more about the narrator's self.

One of the most interesting aspects of "The Ponds" is the way in which the seasonal metaphor is woven into its metaphoric fabric. We have spoken previously of the correlation between the seasons of the year and the "spiritual seasons" of the narrator. As "winter" approaches, the "pond" echoes the changing atmosphere: "It no longer reflected the bright tints of October, but the sombre November colours of the surrounding hills." Later, in the winter chapters of *Walden*, we will see this sombreness reflected in the narrator's self. As the months move on, the pond will be covered with ice; an "icy shutter" will be drawn across its "broad skylight" and, likewise, the narrator's self will be "icy"; an "icy shutter" will be drawn across its "broad skylight" and, like the pond, it will be cut off from "the spirit that is in the air." Then the narrator's ecstasy will dwindle. But he will remain hopeful for he can be sure of a "thaw" in the spring. And the pond will exemplify the basis for believing that his spiritual life will not die: "A bright green weed is brought up on anchors even in midwinter." As natural life survives in Walden even during the winter, so the narrator's supernatural, spiritual life will survive through his "winter"; note that in Christian iconography the anchor is a symbol of hope, and green symbolizes not only hope but vitality. Walden Pond is, then, a symbol which reveals many facets of the narrator's self.

After describing Walden itself, the narrator turns to the other bodies of water in the area. As might be expected, none equals Walden. Flint's Pond is "comparatively shallow" (like the man who owns it) and is "not remarkably pure." Goose Pond is "of small extent." White Pond is a "gem of the woods. . . . a lesser twin of Walden." About Fair-Haven Bay, there is nothing to be said. There is only one Walden—as a literal pond and as a symbol for the narrator's perfected self. This is fitting because there is only one perfected self that the narrator knows of—his self. As he told us in "Economy": "I should not talk so much about myself if there were anybody else whom I knew as well." That nearly the entirety of "The Ponds" is devoted to a description of the metaphor for his self confirms this point.

CHAPTER TEN

Baker Farm

Summary

As the chapter opens, we again see the narrator freely roaming the countryside, enraptured with the beauty of the landscape. It is like a dreamland: pine groves stand "like temples" and a hemlock tree seems "like a pagoda in the midst of the woods." He sees other trees that are vitally alive, "spiring higher and higher . . . fit to stand before Valhalla." Nature is expressing herself everywhere with signs of lush ripeness. The narrator is overwhelmed by such splendor and declares that these sights "make the beholder forget his home with their beauty, and he is dazzled and tempted by nameless other wild forbidden fruits, too fair for mortal taste."

52

From this ecstatic experience of natural beauty, the narrator travels to the drab, dismal hut of John Field, an Irish immigrant and common laborer. John is a bogger who works from sunrise to sunset. He is an "honest, hard-working" man, and his wife is "thinking to improve her condition one day," but at present they lead a tired and dreary life, trying to make ends meet. The narrator attempts to help John by telling him about his own schemes of "economy" and how they can make life more enjoyable. But "John heaved a sigh at this, and his wife stared with arms a-kimbo." John came to America because of the luxuries he could not get in Ireland, and the narrator realizes the vicious circle in which John will probably remain: "As he began with tea, and coffee, and butter, and milk, and beef, he had to work hard to pay for them, and when he worked hard he had to eat hard again to repair the waste of his system." John thought that luxuries are worth his backbreaking labors, but the narrator sadly observes that "he was discontented and wasted his life into the bargain."

The narrator gave up trying to convince John of his self-destructive folly and returned to the concerns of his own happy life. He immediately became exuberant as he "ran down the hill toward the reddening west. . . . determined to "enjoy the land, but own it not." The narrator will not be like the many John Fields of the world who "come tamely home at night only from the next field or street." For him, life is—and will be—an adventure; he refuses to be penned into the dull round of conventional living.

Commentary

This chapter constitutes an ecstatic celebration of what the narrator has discovered by looking into the "pond": he rejoices over his own perfection. Thus at the beginning of this chapter, we are presented with a portrait of a vibrant and vital natural scene which reflects the narrator's powerful sense of spiritual vitality. He again records his happiness, telling us: "Once it chanced that I stood in the very abutment of a rainbow's arch, which filled the lower stratum of the atmosphere, tinging the grass and leaves around, and dazzling me as if I looked through coloured crystal. It was a lake of rainbow light, in which, for a short while, I lived like a dolphin." Within this statement, the narrator informs us of his sublime contentment in three ways: first, he stood at the rainbow's end and was thus the lucky mortal who found the "pot of gold"; second, being flooded in resplendent light symbolizes an experience of spiritual illumination; and third, he compares himself to a dolphin, which is a traditional symbol of immortality. Thoreau makes sure that he has made his point about the narrator's spiritual state with one last touch. He has his narrator declare: "As I walked on the railroad causeway, I used to wonder at the halo of light around my shadow, and would fain fancy myself one of the elect." It is a whimsical, witty statement by the narrator, but it reinforces the claim for spiritual perfection made through the pond symbol of the previous chapter.

CHAPTER ELEVEN

Higher Laws

Summary

While coming home from fishing one night, the narrator was suddenly overwhelmed by a sense of rank, primitive animality, a feeling of wildness. Seeing a woodchuck cross his path, he felt "a strange thrill of savage delight" and was "strongly tempted to seize and devour him raw." This same instinctual urge had come to him previously. At times, he found himself "ranging the woods, like a half-starved hound, with a strange abandonment, seeking some kind of venison which I might devour. The narrator qualifies these somewhat extreme remarks by telling his readers that he was not literally hungry, but that he did strongly desire the experience of wildness, the vicarious feeling of animal existence in nature.

Almost immediately, the narrator tells us of another instinctive urge that he frequently felt: "I found in myself, and still find, an instinct toward a higher, or, as it is named, spiritual life, as do most men." Thus there are two instinctual drives that dominate his personality, and he tells us that he reveres them both: "I love the wild not less than the good." Yet, while this is true, he spends the rest of the chapter explaining how his instinctual animality is not only inferior to, but in conflict with, his inclination toward spirituality.

He explains this problem by focusing on the matter of his nourishment while at Walden Pond. While gradually developing his spiritual faculties, he adopted a diet of ascetic, more spiritual foods. This was a part of his self-purification process, for he had virtually given up hunting and fishing because eating flesh seemed "essentially unclean." Yet, he realized that the animal urge toward flesh was still very much a part of him: "If I were to live in a wilderness I should again be tempted to become a fisher and hunter in earnest." His animal nature can be controlled and lessened, but it cannot be eradicated — "possibly we may withdraw from it, but never change its nature."

The narrator believes, however, that he and all men are gradually evolving through time toward a more spiritual, less animal, state. "Whatever my own practice may be," he says, "I have no doubt that it is a part of the destiny of the human race, in its gradual improvement, to leave off eating animals." To give a concrete illustration of this point, he tells us how he once, in his youth, greatly delighted in hunting. In fact, he still believes that it is a very valuable activity for young men because it brings them in close contact with nature. Because of this contact, the narrator gradually gave up hunting for animals in nature and began to "hunt" for higher, more spiritual "game." He sees this change in his own interests as natural in a man's growth process, and he advises parents to encourage such growth in their boys: "*Make* them hunters, though sportsmen only at first; if possible, mighty hunters at last, so that they shall not find game large enough for them in this or any vegetable wilderness — hunters as well as fishers of men." Some day they will bag spiritual truths, higher laws, instead of woodchucks and rabbits. Once the individual lessens his animality, as the narrator was able to do, his spiritual purity will be increased and he will come to his perfection.

Commentary

"Nature is hard to be overcome, but she must be overcome." This statement, and indeed the entire chapter, may surprise the careful reader who recalls the celebration of the woodchopper's animality and the narrator's happy claim, made at the beginning of "The Ponds," that he has successfully integrated nature and spirit in his self. All of a sudden, the narrator is now declaring the superiority of spirit over nature and the incompatability of spirituality and animality, in this chapter, the worlds of spirit and nature are put at odds. In short, the narrator's self is once again confronting a dialectical situation—which, again, must be resolved if his vision of life is to remain an integrated one. For while spirit is higher than nature, the narrator will not give up his vital relationship with nature; somehow, he must reconcile the apparent opposition between his spiritual instincts and his animal instincts.

To Thoreau, as well as to Emerson and other transcendentalists, nature reveals absolute truths. Therefore, we find the narrator turning to natural phenomena for an answer to his problem. Nature immediately confirms his belief that animality in man is opposed to spiritual perfection. He learns this by focusing on the life cycle of a butterfly. The butterfly, in its perfect state of fulfillment as a creature, eats very little, whereas the imperfect larva of the butterfly consumes every edible bit that it finds. From this, the narrator "skims off" a truth for man: "the gross feeder is a man in the larva state," while the ascetic individual is in his "butterfly" state, his state of perfection.

As may be noted, the narrator has not resolved the conflict between animality and spirituality. His examination of a particular natural phenomenon has only strengthened the conviction that "every man who has ever been earnest to preserve his higher or poetic faculties in the best condition has been particularly inclined to abstain from animal food." Upon a closer consideration of the butterfly, however, the narrator seems to find the key to his dilemma: "The abdomen under the wings of the butterfly still represents the larva." In the perfected body of the butterfly is integrated the lower state of his life *and* the higher. Here is what the narrator may be able to do. He may be able to perfect his lowly animal nature to the point at which it will not conflict with his spiritual nature. Since "we are all sculptors and painters, and our material is our own flesh and blood and bones," the body may be fashioned into a fit "temple" for the inner spiritual self. As the spiritual self is perfected, the "temple" will eventually be refined from within and physically show perfection.

CHAPTER TWELVE

Brute Neighbours

Summary

The chapter opens with a dramatic dialogue between a Hermit (who seems to represent the narrator) and a Poet. The Hermit sits alone and muses upon a familiar question: "Why will men worry themselves so? He that does not eat need not work." The Poet approaches him and asks if he would like to go fishing, "the true industry for poets." The Hermit seriously considers the proposition. Should he continue his meditation or fish with his friend? "Shall I go to heaven or a-fishing?" Eventually he decides to fish and goes off with the Poet, leaving his deep thoughts for another time.

After this dialogue is completed, the narrator describes the various animals, the "brute neighbours," that harmoniously lived with him at Walden. There is the friendly mouse that climbed up his sleeves and gobbled the crumbs given him. A phoebe built her nest in his shed and a robin dwelt in the pine tree next to his cabin. Partridges filed beneath his window, and beyond his window the woods were busy with animal activity. The narrator gives us lively descriptions of otters, racoons, woodcocks, turtledoves, squirrels, jays, and many other animals. In such a setting, his ability to perceive natural phenomena was developed to such an extent that he was able to observe and depict in minute detail a battle between red and black ants near his woodpile. While he was doing this, his imagination was so stimulated that he turned the ant fight into an epic war between "the red republicans" and "the black imperialists"—and thus he "skimmed off" another truth for man: is a war between ants any more or any less significant than one between men?

The loon that the narrator observed swimming in Walden Pond is of special interest. He spent much time observing him, listening to his wild, laughing cries, and occasionally rowed out to try and catch him. The ducks that circled above the pond in the autumn also provided a spectacle worth hours of observation.

Commentary

It seemed at the end of "Higher Laws" that the narrator had resolved the conflict between his animality and spirituality. Yet the dialogue which begins this chapter indicates that he is still troubled by it. The Hermit and the Poet represent the two instinctual sides of the narrator. We should note that when the Poet invites the Hermit to go fishing (an animalistic activity) the Hermit must completely abandon his higher thoughts in order to do so—in spite of the fact that he is "as near [to] being resolved into the essence of things" as he ever was in his life. Thus, through this dialogue, Thoreau is restating the incompatability of spiritual consciousness and animalistic activity. For the narrator to follow his animal instincts by fishing, he must disengage himself from spiritual activity; the narrator finds it an "either-or" choice that he must make. He cannot follow both his animal and his spiritual instincts at the same time.

Still very much interested in integrating the two instincts, the narrator turns to nature again for a solution—and he finds it. He sees the partridge, the "winged cat," and the loon as natural symbols of how spirituality and animality can be integrated. The partridge provides an example of how animality can be perfected to the point at which it complements spirituality. In the partridge, the narrator finds perfected animality: "so perfect is this instinct." And in this creature he also finds a sign of perfected spirituality. The narrator focuses on the bird's eyes, and in reading his description, we should recall the description of another symbol of spiritual perfection, the "earth's eye," Walden Pond: "All intelligence seems reflected in them. They suggest not merely the purity of infancy, but a wisdom clarified by experience. Such an eye was not born when the bird was, but is coeval with the sky it reflects. The woods do not yield another such a gem. The traveller does not often look into such a limpid well." The "winged cat" reveals a similar truth to the narrator. This cat is one that roams the Walden woods; she has hair so thick that it creates the appearance of wings. Thus, while remaining a wild animal, she signifies spirituality since "wings" indicate spiritual perfection (another example is the hawks in "The Bean-field").

In the loon, the integration of the animal and the spiritual is also seen. The loon in Walden Pond is certainly wild, and that he is more than merely wild is revealed by the narrator's word choices. Describing the cry of the loon, the narrator speaks of his "unearthly laugh," his "long-drawn unearthly howl," and his "demoniac laughter." One scene especially suggests the narrator's perception of the loon: "He uttered one of those prolonged howls, as if calling on the god of loons to aid him, and immediately there came a wind from the east and rippled the surface, and filled the whole air with misty rain . . . as if it were the prayer of the loon answered, and his god was angry with me, and so I left him disappearing far away on the tumultuous surface."

Through these three symbols, nature indicates to the narrator that animality and spirituality need not be in conflict. But while the narrator sees this in nature, it seems as though he is not yet able to resolve the conflict within himself. This failure on the part of the narrator is dramatically expressed in his unsuccessful attempt at catching the loon—the loon being a symbol for the narrator's ideal, perfected self. The loon took on this symbolic meaning when Thoreau described it in terms of purification and rebirth: "In the fall the loon came, as usual, to moult and bathe in the pond." This symbolism was further developed when the loon became a sign of animal and spiritual integration. Hence, the loon represents those ideal qualities that the narrator wants to possess in his personality. His failure to "catch" the loon signifies his failure to develop those qualities in himself.

After considering the above point, it would seem that the narrator was a bit premature in claiming his perfection in "The Ponds" and "Baker Farm." This is the second time that the narrator has failed to resolve a dialectical situation. Much earlier he could not integrate the worlds of nature and the machine (signified by the locomotive); now he cannot integrate two powerful instincts within him. The reader should note that the narrator has seemingly forgotten his first failure; and the reader should also note that the narrator will forget this second failure. Both failures will be ignored by the end of *Walden* when the narrator will be caught up in an incandescently ecstatic celebration of nature's spring rebirth, and his own consequent spiritual rebirth.

CHAPTER THIRTEEN

House-warming

Summary

October arrived and the narrator began to prepare for the winter months. While admiring the brilliant autumn foliage, he gathered grapes, collected half a bushel of chestnuts, and brought in a small store of wild apples for coddling. Gradually the weather got colder, and when the wasps began flocking into his cabin to hibernate, the narrator decided it was time to move indoors to the warmth of his hearth.

He describes at length how he built his chimney, "the most vital part of the house." As is usual with the narrator, this employment proved to be a source of great enjoyment. He cleansed his second-hand bricks, mixed his own mortar with sand from Walden, and happily engaged himself in the art of masonry. Throughout the winter, the fire in the hearth was like a friend; and once he had finished plastering its walls, the cabin became a comfortable "shell" into which he could withdraw.

While the narrator was completing his cabin, the pond began to freeze. The narrator welcomed the first ice and spent hours studying the bottom of the pond through the glasslike ice, viewing the furrows in the sand, the cases of cadis worms, and other interesting objects. But the ice itself was "the object of most interest." This was so because of the designs which the bubbles formed beneath it. The delight he received from viewing them may be gleaned from the language he uses to describe them: "They were no longer one directly over another, but often like silvery coins poured from a bag, one overlapping another."

Having told us about the beauty of the pond and the comfort of his cabin, the narrator thus begins the story of the winter he spent at Walden Pond.

Commentary

After reading this chapter, one would probably not guess that it reveals the beginning of a crisis in the narrator's life. It is only after reading the next three chapters, the so-called winter chapters, that one can see that "House-warming" introduces the narrator's spiritual trial. Until now, we have seen the narrator happily living through the spring and summer—the seasons of nature's rebirth and fruition and the narrator's spiritual seasons of rebirth and maturation. Inspired by natural influences, he has been renewed and vitalized. Now, with nature's season of inactivity fast approaching, natural stimuli are being removed from the narrator's experience. Without external stimuli to keep up his spirits, he had to depend solely on himself for spiritual survival. He had to turn inward—metaphorically indicated by his preparations to move indoors—and keep alive his spirit with the strength he has "stored up" within his soul. As fall moved into winter, "the character of each tree came out"; likewise, the narrator's true character will "come out" and its spiritual strength will be tested. As the "winter set in in good earnest," the narrator prepared to preserve his spiritual life: "I withdrew yet farther into my shell, and endeavoured to keep a bright fire both within my house and within my breast."

This "fire" within his breast is a traditional symbol of inspiration, and when the narrator uses this symbol he prods the reader into realizing the spiritual significance of the fireplace and the chimney that he has built in preparation for winter. As a fireplace is necessary to keep an actual fire within the cabin, a spiritually strong self is needed to preserve the "fire" of inspiration. Hence, in building his chimney, the narrator is metaphorically describing his final attempt "to build" a spiritually strong soul that can contain the "fire." With this in mind, we can see the metaphorical significance of one particular description of the chimney. Like the narrator's soul, "the chimney is to some extent an independent structure, standing on the ground and rising through the house to the heavens; even after the house is burned it still stands sometimes." Thus Thoreau metaphorically links the house and chimney with the narrator's body and soul. That the narrator is describing his last attempt at strengthening his spirit is again indicated by his *purifying* the bricks for the chimney by scraping and washing them; moreover, it is no accident that he uses the terminology of spiritual rebirth when discussing the construction of his hearth: "I was surprised to see . . . how many pailfuls of water it takes to christen a new hearth." How many times already have we seen the narrator "baptize" his self, using much the same language to describe the process?

In the next three chapters, we will see how successfully the narrator has strengthened his soul so that it can survive a spiritual "winter."

CHAPTER FOURTEEN

Former Inhabitants; and Winter Visitors

Summary

This chapter begins with the narrator attempting to preserve his happy, summer state of mind in the midst of winter. He buoyantly tells us, "I weathered some merry snow storms, and spent some cheerful winter evenings by my fireside." Yet, while making the best of his situation, it is not long before we hear a sombre note in the narrator's voice. All nature is silent and still—"even the hooting of the owl was hushed"—and, indirectly, he is telling us that he received no natural stimulation. The deep snow made visits from friends less frequent and, in this solitary situation, he had to exercise his ingenuity to keep his mind active: "For human society I was obliged to conjure up the former occupants of these woods." Turning to memory and history to keep his mind busy, he describes the former inhabitants of the Walden area.

He recounts the residences of three former slaves: Cato Ingraham, whose Walden land was eventually taken away by "a younger and whiter speculator"; Zilpha, an elderly woman who spun linen and made the woods ring with her songs; and Brister Freeman, whose wife, Fenda, "pleasantly" told fortunes. There is the ruined farm of the Stratten family, and also the Breed's house, which was burnt to the ground not long ago by mischievous children. The narrator recalls that he had been shown the Breed's place by one of the family. This fellow was especially gratified to find that the well had not been destroyed, but was merely covered up and could again be tapped someday.

When considering the remains of Hugh Quoil's place, the narrator again focuses on a covered well. It makes him feel melancholy that "where once a spring oozed" there is now "dry and tearless grass." Such recollections make the narrator sad, and he gives them up for comforting sleep.

Since there were hardly any visitors, the narrator spent much time walking across the winter landscape, observing the snow-covered trees and an occasional animal. One time, he came upon a drowsy owl perched on the dead limb of a pine. The owl seemed as inactive as the rest of nature, but the narrator found this appearance to be deceiving when he moved too close to the owl. The owl abruptly came to life: "He launched himself off, and flapped through the pines, spreading his wings to unexpected breadth." Strolling farther, the narrator found other signs of nature's continuing vitality in the midst of winter.

When the narrator returned to his cabin from these jaunts, he sometimes found a friend waiting for him. Once, a "long-headed farmer" visited him, and they heartily recalled "rude and simple times, when men sat about large fires in cold, bracing weather, with clear heads." A poet also visited him and together they made "that small house ring with boisterous mirth and resound with the murmur of much sober talk." A philosopher also stopped by. He was a great, ideal man whose personality made "plain the image engraven in men's bodies, the God of whom they are but defaced and leaning monuments." The narrator was inspired by his conversation with the philosopher and felt a heightened spiritual awareness.

Commentary

In this chapter, the narrator turns to three possible sources of spiritual stimulation. The first, history, proved to be unstimulating, and even depressing. Finally he gave it up, declaring, "Alas! how little does the memory of these human inhabitants enhance the beauty of the landscape!" In considering this first part of the chapter, we should note a symbol which appears twice — the covered-up wells of the Breed place and the Quoil place. As was mentioned in the commentary on "The Ponds," springs and wells are often-used symbols for inspiration. That these particular wells are covered up and no longer flow indicates that the narrator's inspiration has been cut off in this spiritual "winter." It is significant, however, that the wells are merely covered up and that they are not destroyed; this signifies the hope of the narrator that he may once again "uncover" and tap his "well" of inspiration.

When the narrator turns from history to nature, the second possible source of stimulation, we again see him looking for confirmation of his hope that his spiritual life will not die. When he saw the owl, he observed a sign of torpidity in nature that reflected his own spiritual torpidity. But when the owl burst into flight, nature showed the narrator that there was still vitality in nature beneath the appearance of lifelessness; nature did not die simply because of winter. Watching the owl and discovering the skunk-cabbages which still grew in the swamps in winter, the narrator was taught by nature that he need not die spiritually

simply because he was experiencing a psychological "winter."
This realization did not produce ecstasy in the narrator, but it
did give him hope for spiritual survival. Like the "hardier bird"
in the swamp, he hopefully awaited the return of spring.

After reading such chapters as "Solitude," "Visitors," and
"The Village," the reader will find it ironic that the final, possible source of stimulation, human company, is the most vitaliz-
ing one. To the narrator, the philosopher made heaven and earth
meet; he produced a sense of ecstatic integration in the narrator's
spiritual "winter."

CHAPTER FIFTEEN

Winter Animals

Summary

With all of the ponds in the area frozen, the narrator found
new and shorter routes by which to roam the countryside. Most
important, by standing in the middle of ponds such as Flint's, he
was able to scan the landscape from unique points of view. Thus,
on this "snowy plain," he could imaginatively enjoy the countryside's new appearance. Yet, after a moment of enjoyment, a
sombre note returns to the narrator's voice. He tells us that on
winter nights the forlorn, melancholy notes of the owl resounded
"indefinitely far." The owls' lonely cries would on some nights
be interrupted by the honking of geese that circled over the
pond. "It was one of the most thrilling discords I ever heard."

The narrator turns our attention to the plentiful wildlife that
moved through the snowy woods. Some nights he would hear
foxes ranging over the crusty snow; red squirrels scampered over
his roof, jays screamed from the tree tops; and chickadees pecked
at the crumbs placed before the cabin door. Hounds bellowed
far off in the hills, chasing a fox.

One day the narrator encountered a hare in pitiful condition.
The narrator was depressed to encounter such a wretched sight

in nature, but then he received a welcome surprise: "I took a step, and lo, away it scud with an elastic spring over the snow crust, straightening its body and its limits into graceful length, and soon put the forest between me and itself—the wild free venison, asserting its vigour and the dignity of Nature."

Commentary

The narrator's depressed state is once again revealed, as it was momentarily in "Sounds," by the forlorn hooting of owls in the night. Yet, note that the narrator is struggling to overcome his melancholy. This is indicated when, at the same time that the owls are droning their mournful tones, the circling geese respond with their happier tones (recall that flying birds signify spiritual elevation). The narrator is not surrendering to his "winter" state of mind, but he is becoming anxious, as is indicated by his description of the symbol for his self, Walden Pond. His restlessness is depicted when he tells us: "I . . . heard the whooping of the ice in the pond . . . as if it were restless in its bed and would fain turn over—were troubled with flatulency and bad dreams." That he is spiritually "low" is shown by the rest of the chapter, in which there are no touchings of heaven and earth, no mystical unions with nature and the divine—in short, no signs of the contentment that characterized the spring and summer chapters. Only once is there a truly optimistic note sounded, and that is when the "dropsical" rabbit suddenly reasserts the continuing vitality of nature that survives beneath the appearance of death. As in the case with the drowsy owl in the previous chapter, the narrator is again taught by nature that he need not spiritually die during his psychological "winter."

CHAPTER SIXTEEN

The Pond in Winter

Summary

One winter morning the narrator woke somewhat confused from a restless and troubled sleep: "I awoke with the impression that some question had been put to me, which I had been endeavouring in vain to answer in my sleep, as what—how—when —where?" It has been a long winter; he has been anxious and disturbed about his spiritual life. That morning he looked out of his window and rediscovered the answer to all of his worries and questions: "There was dawning Nature, in whom all creatures live, looking in at my broad windows with serene and satisfied face, and no question on *her* lips. I awoke to an answered question, to Nature and daylight." He obeyed nature's unspoken command, "Forward!" and began to move out of his wintry spiritual state of despondency. Imbued with a new sense of vitality, he energetically began his morning work by taking his pail to the pond and searching for water beneath the ice and snow.

He cut a hole in the ice and, while drawing water, enjoyed looking through this "window" into the depths below. Soon he caught a glimpse of the life moving below the ice. He was overjoyed with the sight and exclaimed, "Ah, the pickerel of Walden! . . . I am always surprised by their rare beauty, as if they were fabulous fishes. . . . They possess a quite dazzling and transcendent beauty."

The narrator then tells us that in the late winter of 1846, before the ice broke up, he measured the depth and charted the topography of the pond's bottom. He found that Walden, which was previously thought to be "bottomless," was one hundred and seven feet deep. Relating this fact to his own spiritual interests, he declares, "This is a remarkable depth for so small an area; yet not an inch of it can be spared by the imagination. What if all ponds were shallow? Would it not react on the minds of men? I am thankful that this pond was made deep and pure for a symbol."

One January day, the narrator looked out at the pond and saw a crew of a hundred Irish laborers and Yankee foremen cutting out the Walden ice for sale in warmer weather and in southern climates. At first, he was upset at the thought of their stealing Walden's "skin"; but, upon reflection, he gladdened at the thought of the sweltering inhabitants of Charleston, New

Orleans, Bombay, and Calcutta drinking at his Walden "well." The moral is obvious; he hopes that they can derive the great value from Walden that he has.

In concluding the chapter, the narrator tells us that in the mornings he would "bathe" his intellect "in the stupendous and cosmogonal philosophy of the Bhagvat Geeta." This would send him into an imaginative revery and he would feel as though he had integrated Oriental and Western thought and culture on the shores of Walden. Thus the "pure Walden water [was] mingled with the sacred water of the Ganges."

Commentary

When reading this chapter, one immediately notes how much more vigorous the narrator has become. In "Former Inhabitants; and Winter Visitors" and in "Winter Animals" we saw him straining to find sources of spiritual stimulation; with the beginning of this chapter, his quest seems to be over. He is inspired once again by the "serene and satisfied face of Nature." Upon receiving new inspiration, his first actions are symbolically revealing. He goes to the pond (the symbol for his self) and cuts away the ice ("cuts through" his wintry psychological state). Looking into the depths of the pond, thus metaphorically looking within his soul, he rejoices over a world of incomparable beauty. What he sees in the literal pond is pickerel possessing "transcendent beauty." These pickerel signify the narrator's own thoughts which he finds to be transcendently beautiful.

In discussing the depth of Walden and how Walden is like a "deep" symbol, the narrator again indicates that his imagination was "thawing" and was now active. His concluding statements about Walden ice being shipped to southern climates and about mixing Ganges water with Walden water indicate that his imagination is stimulated. Metaphorically, he depicts a feeling of oneness with the people of different countries, with the thought of different cultures and philosophies, and with the people and thought of past centuries. He is depicting a feeling of integration with all things on earth—in the past and present.

Yet winter is still upon the narrator; he is not totally "awake." He tells us that Walden still has its "eyelids" closed; accordingly, his soul has still not regained its full spiritual vision. Spring, in the literal and the symbolic sense, has not yet come. And the narrator looks forward to and longs for its arrival: "In thirty days more, probably, I shall look from the same window on the pure sea-green Walden water."

CHAPTER SEVENTEEN

Spring

Summary

Winter finally passed, and spring came in, dramatically announced by the audible breaking-up of the Walden ice. The narrator felt his own spiritual "thaw" and revitalization coming on, and he further describes the pond's thaw in terms of this feeling — "it stretched itself and yawned like a waking man with a gradually increasing tumult." It was not many days before the thaw was completed in the pond; soon all of nature surrounding the pond began to show signs of its annual rebirth. And as would be expected, the narrator grew ecstatic as he witnessed these signs of nature's new vitality.

One phenomenon of nature's thaw which particularly stimulated the narrator's imagination occurred in the railroad bank that ran along one side of the pond. As he viewed the thawing sand and clay flowing down the bank like lava, running into various forms, it seemed as though nature was visibly expressing its new life, as though organic, living things are being created out of inorganic, dead matter. Thus he came to feel that the world was once again being created, as though for the first time. The narrator keenly feels that he was deeply involved in this rebirth, this re-creation, for what is the truly inspired man "but a mass of thawing clay" flowing out of his wintry state of spiritual frigidity and rigidity into a new form of life?

Turning to other scenes in the revitalized landscape, he tells us that he came upon other poignant signs of nature's rebirth, such as the first sparrow of spring and a slight and graceful hawk and a marsh hawk. As the day moved into evening the narrator was suddenly startled by the honking of the returning geese that flew low over the woods.

Looking then at the vegetation, he saw that the pitch-pines and shrub-oaks which had drooped through the winter had suddenly become greener, more erect and alive. By May, nature's new, rich fertility fully expressed itself. Even the lowly grasses revealed nature's new vigor. From the image of "springing" grass, the narrator "skims off" another truth about his present feeling of new vitality: "our human life but dies down to its root, and still puts forth its green blade to eternity."

The narrator is once again ecstatic in nature and he concludes the chapter by succinctly summarizing the sense of strong vitality continuously showing forth in nature. "And so the seasons went rolling on into summer, as one rambles into higher and higher grass." As nature grows toward its summer maturation, the narrator will grow toward his spiritual fulfillment.

Commentary

Two symbolic statements are made by the narrator which seem to be the theme of this chapter: "Walden was dead and is alive again" and "It is glorious to behold this ribbon of water sparkling in the sun, the bare face of the pond full of glee and youth." As we already know, the pond is a symbol for the narrator's self, and these statements — and, indeed, the entire chapter — symbolize the happy rebirth of the narrator's spirit. Like "The Ponds," this chapter is a highly compressed collage of metaphors and symbols which reveal the narrator's glowing feeling of spiritual elevation. It would be difficult to find one sentence in this chapter which does not fulfill this function.

In a final paragraph, the narrator informs us that he left Walden Pond on September 6, 1847. And, although the narrator earlier informed us that he left the pond because he had other lives to lead, it is not inappropriate to wonder why he *did* leave this marvelous world that he describes in these chapters. Some critics believe that Thoreau's actual experience at the pond was not as successful as the narrator's experience in *Walden* — a point which serves to emphasize the fact that *Walden* is an imaginative, artistic creation and not a strict biographical account of life in the woods.

CHAPTER EIGHTEEN

Conclusion

Summary and *Commentary*

The experiment and spiritual quest at Walden Pond is concluded and, based upon the truths discovered and revealed, the narrator makes a final exhortation that his readers also begin a new and finer life. He tells us that just because we live in such and such a town, within four walls, we should not conclude that our lives must be limited, shallow, and ordinary. Nor need we travel around the world to have an interesting life. Life can be an enriching "voyage," not necessarily involving the exploration of darkest Africa or the South Seas. Rather, the rich life involves an *inward* voyage whereby we discover our divine potentialities, our unique possibilities for greatness as men. He advises his readers thus:

> Direct your eye right inward, and you'll find
> A thousand regions in your mind
> Yet undiscovered. Travel them, and be
> Expert in home-cosmography.

Against the background of contemporary American expansionism, he wonders why so many men trifle away their lives in geographical exploration: "What does Africa — what does the West stand for? Is not our own interior white on the chart/ . . . Obey the precept of the old philosopher, and Explore thyself"; there are "continents and seas in the moral world, to which every man is an isthmus or an inlet, yet unexplored by him."

Once one discovers what is within the self, he should then construct a vision of how he can develop the potentiality for the greatness that he finds. Man can become whatever he chooses to be. His potential is vast and is able to be realized in this life; the narrator is convinced that "if one advances confidently in the direction of his dreams, and endeavours to live the life which he has imagined, he will meet with a success unexpected in common hours." He offers us this view of ourselves and warns us not to fall into the "democratic" trap of being content with remaining "common men" and priding ourselves on being merely "average Americans" who live by that much overrated commodity, common sense. "Why level downward to our dullest perception always, and praise that as common-sense. The commonest sense is the sense of men asleep, which they express by snoring."

He tells us to avoid the paralyzing influence of the past and *not* to listen to those who are constantly "dinning in our ears that we Americans, and moderns generally, are intellectual dwarfs compared with the ancients, or even the Elizabethan men." We should not spend our time worrying about the so-called good old days, when "men were men": "Let every one mind his own business, and endeavour to be what he was made."

Conformity is another trap to avoid: "Why should we be in such desperate haste to succeed, and in such desperate enterprises? If a man does not keep pace with his companions, perhaps it is because he hears a different drummer. Let him step to the music which he hears, however measured or far away." Inner exploration and growth are the personal concerns of each unique individual; each must discover his own truths and live by them accordingly. The narrator has offered us the example of how this may be done; we have seen him decide "not to live in this restless, nervous, bustling, trivial Nineteenth Century, but stand or sit thoughtfully while it goes by" and tend to his own self-cultivation.

The result of such a way of living is illustrated by the fable of the "strong and beautiful bug" with which the narrator ends *Walden*. Fittingly, *Walden* concludes with an emphatic note of optimism and hope in man's ability to transcend his self-imposed limitations and fulfill his unmeasured potential for excellence.

EXTRA-LITERARY RECOGNITION OF THOREAU

Although studies of Thoreau by such twentieth-century scholars as F. O. Matthiessen, Sherman Paul, and Walter Harding have made his writings very popular in university and literary circles, the often hard-hitting truths that Thoreau presents in his books and essays have attracted by themselves a widespread audience. Dr. Martin Luther King, Jr. acknowledged his personal debt to Thoreau's thought-provoking essay on civil disobedience by declaring that, "I was so deeply moved that I re-read the work ["Civil Disobedience"] several times. . . . No other person has been more eloquent and passionate in getting this idea across than Henry David Thoreau. As a result of his writings and personal witness, we are heirs of a legacy of creative protest." In India, another civil rights leader, Mohandas Gandhi, was also stimulated by Thoreau's writings. Gandhi admitted that "his ideas influenced me greatly. I adopted some of them and recommended the study of Thoreau to all my friends who were helping me in the cause of Indian independence. . . . There is no doubt that Thoreau's ideas greatly influenced my movement in India." In 1962, Rev. Trevor Bush, a leader in the protest movement against the racist policies of the South African government, also acknowledged a similar indebtedness to Thoreau: "His influence in South Africa has been extremely important and our struggle to win rights for the oppressed non-white population of our country has been assisted profoundly by the fearless liberal teachings and example of . . . [this] great philosopher and prophet." These are only a few of many examples of Thoreau's influence on social action in America and abroad, and his consequent popularity. It is likely that Thoreau will continue to have a large audience among those who are searching for timeless truths that can be applied to man's situation. As philosopher Martin Buber has pointed out: "Thoreau expresses exactly that which is valid for all human history." In Thoreau's writings, one may discover that literature may be very much connected with real-life needs; one may find that art can be immediately relevant to everyday personal and social concerns.

One of the most extraordinary instances in which the popular appeal of Thoreau's thought has been recognized is related by Walter Harding in *The Variorum Civil Disobedience*. Citing examples of official resistance to Thoreau, Harding writes that, "when, in the mid-1950s, the United States Information Service included as a standard book in all their libraries around the world a textbook of American literature which reprinted Thoreau's 'Civil Disobedience,' the late Senator Joseph McCarthy of Wisconsin succeeded in having that book removed from the shelves of those libraries — specifically because of the Thoreau essay."

As may be seen, Thoreau has not been ignored during the twentieth century, by either friend or foe. The twentieth-century mind, whether in agreement or disagreement with Thoreau, has found in his writings an engaging intellectual challenge which cannot be ignored. In his anti-materialism, his transcendental optimism about the nature of man, and his view of society, Thoreau sharply questions the basic assumptions of modern American life. In *Walden* and "Civil Disobedience," Thoreau asks the "hard questions" about the way in which modern man lives, and they are questions that may be only temporarily avoided by intelligent men. Sooner or later, one must formulate a position in regard to Thoreau's view of the relationship between the individual and the state as expressed in "Civil Disobedience." Eventually, one must evaluate the anti-materialistic, spiritual view of life found in *Walden*. Thoreau's writings strongly invite us to think and respond; and in this lies a main cause for much of his present popularity.

ESSAY QUESTIONS AND THEME TOPICS

1. How is *Walden* an expression of the transcendentalist vision?

2. Is the claim that the narrator of *Walden* is an anti-social recluse a valid one?

3. Describe how the narrator's financial "economy" is expanded to a philosophy of life.

4. What makes *Walden* a unified work of art rather than a "collection of eighteen essays"?

5. Discuss the seasonal metaphor that thematically unifies *Walden*.

6. Consider the significance of Walden Pond as a symbol.

7. What is John Field's debilitating problem?

8. Discuss the narrator's attitude toward the state.

9. Describe the narrator's reaction to the railroad.

10. What is the significance of the spring thaw at the railroad cut?

11. As described in *Walden*, what is wrong with American culture?

12. Discuss the significance of the narrator's bean-field.

13. Discuss the significance of Thoreau's use of the "I" voice in *Walden*.

SELECTED BIBLIOGRAPHY

ANDERSON, CHARLES R. *The Magic Circle of Walden*. New York: Holt, Rinehart, and Winston, 1968. Treats *Walden* as a successful, unified poem. It is one of the best studies of *Walden* as a work of art.

75

GLICK, WENDELL, ed. *The Recognition of Henry David Thoreau.* Ann Arbor: University of Michigan Press, 1969. A collection of critical essays since 1848 which reveals the gradual recognition of Thoreau.

HARDING, WALTER. *The Days of Henry Thoreau.* New York: Alfred A. Knopf, 1965. The definitive biography.

———, ed. *The Thoreau Centennial.* Yellow Springs, Ohio: Antioch Press, 1965. Essays viewing Thoreau's significance a century after his death.

———. *A Thoreau Handbook.* New York: New York University Press. A guide to research on Thoreau. Also includes critical and biographical essays by Harding.

LANE, LAURIAT. *Approaches to Walden.* San Francisco: Wadsworth, 1961. A very useful guide for beginning a study of *Walden.* Contains critical evaluations, historical data relevant to the writings of *Walden,* and reactions to *Walden.*

MELTZER, MILTON, ed. *Thoreau: People, Principles, and Politics.* New York: Hill and Wang, 1963. An excellent anthology of Thoreau's social writings. Includes journal entries and most of Thoreau's essays of social criticism.

MILLER, PERRY, ed. *Consciousness in Concord.* Boston: Houghton Mifflin, 1958. Presents for the first time Thoreau's journal of 1840-41. Lengthy introduction closely studies the unattractive side of Thoreau's personality.

PAUL, SHERMAN, ed. *Thoreau: A Collection of Critical Essays.* Englewood Cliffs, N.J.: Prentice-Hall, 1962. A collection of essays on various aspects of Thoreau's thoughts and writings.

———. *The Shores of America: Thoreau's Inward Exploration.* Urbana: University of Illinois Press, 1958. A literary-biographical study of Thoreau. The finest of its kind.

———, ed. *Walden* and *Civil Disobedience*. Boston: Houghton Mifflin, 1957. Contains an excellent critical introduction to both texts.

RULAND, RICHARD, ed. *Twentieth Century Interpretations of Walden*. Englewood Cliffs, N.J.: Prentice-Hall, 1968. A collection of critical essays on *Walden*.

SHANLEY, J. LYNDON. *The Making of Walden*. Chicago: University of Chicago Press, 1957. A collection of the successive revisions of the *Walden* manuscripts.

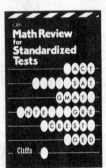 

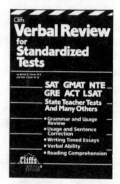